LITTLE HOUSE · BIG ADVENTURE
LITTLE HOUSE

THE LITTLE HOUSE
GUIDEBOOK

by **WILLIAM ANDERSON**

photographs by **LESLIE A. KELLY**

Collins

An Imprint of HarperCollins*Publishers*

Black-and-white maps by Patricia Tobin
Full-color map by Deborah A. Maze
Collins is an imprint of HarperCollins Publishers.

Little House® is a trademark of HarperCollins Publishers.

The Little House Guidebook
Copyright © 1996 by William Anderson
Photographs copyright © 1996, 2007 by Leslie A. Kelly
Photo on page 51 © Laura Ingalls Wilder Memorial Society, De Smet, SD
Photo on page 79 by permission of Laura Ingalls Wilder Home Association
Photos on pages 39, 77 courtesy of William Anderson
Manufactured in Hong Kong. For information address HarperCollins Children's Books, a division of
HarperCollins Publishers, 195 Broadway, New York, NY 10007.
www.littlehousebooks.com

Library of Congress Cataloging-in-Publication Data
Anderson, William, date
The Little House guidebook / by William Anderson; photographs by Leslie A. Kelly.
p. cm.
Includes index.
Summary: A comprehensive guidebook to all the homes in which Laura Ingalls Wilder once lived
and which have now been preserved as historic landmarks and museums.
ISBN-10: 0-06-125512-2 — ISBN-13: 978-0-06-125512-0
1. Wilder, Laura Ingalls, 1867–1957—Homes and haunts—Guidebooks. 2. Women authors,
American—Homes and haunts—Guidebooks. 3. Literary landmarks—United States—Guidebooks.
4. Frontier and pioneer life—United States. [1. Wilder, Laura Ingalls, 1867–1957—Homes and
haunts. 2. Authors, American—Homes and haunts. 3. Frontier and pioneer life—United States.]
1. Kelly, Leslie A., ill.
PS3545.I342Z559 1996   95-33200
813'.52—dc20   CIP
                                                                                                                  AC

Design by Andrea Vandergrift
16 PX 10 9 8 7

Third edition, 2007

CONTENTS

 # INTRODUCTION

When Laura Ingalls Wilder wrote her Little House books in the 1930s and 1940s, she had no idea that she would make either herself or her frontier homes famous. She wrote her books simply to preserve the stories of her pioneer girlhood and her family's covered wagon journeys west during the 1870s and 1880s. But her books rang so true that readers immediately longed to know more about the people and the places on the pages.

Some readers came to visit Laura herself, stopping at her Rocky Ridge Farm in Mansfield, Missouri. One family of Little House readers came knocking on the farmhouse door at seven in the morning, causing Laura to joke that the summer tourists outdid even farmers in early rising.

Thousands of people also wrote to Laura, saying how much they loved her Little House books. Laura was often asked in these letters about her former homesites, which stretched from the Big Woods near Pepin, Wisconsin, to the plains of De Smet, South Dakota. "I had no idea I was writing history," the author commented when she realized the intense interest in her little houses.

Laura lived to know that the settings of her stories were becoming literary and historic landmarks. As early as 1948, a California mother wrote to tell of her family's stop at De Smet, South Dakota, the site of Laura's *The Long Winter*, *Little Town on the Prairie*, and *These Happy Golden Years*. This mother wrote:

> *We all felt we simply couldn't pass De Smet without trying to*

find out something about your family. As we drove down the main street, the boys kept wondering which building had been "Pa's store." My husband parked the car, saying: "And now?"

I got out and walked down the street where three ladies were visiting in front of a store. I told them what I wanted and I could hardly believe my ears, for one of them, Mrs. Sterr, knew your family. She showed us old pictures, dishes and trunks from your parents' house. She let each of the boys take a button from Ma's sewing box and their joy knew no bound! Another lady then drove with us to the house where you had lived.

Today, the visits to Laura's little houses still continue. Through the years, dedicated people in the many towns Laura lived near or wrote about have worked to preserve and re-create the roots and remembrances of Laura Ingalls Wilder. Now, a network of museums, restored homes, and memorials thrives at each Little House site.

The Little House Guidebook is meant for those Little House fans who would like to visit the Little House sites, or who would simply like to learn more about them. There is a chapter devoted to the sites of each of the little houses Laura wrote about, and to each of the sites Laura lived in but did not write about, such as Rocky Ridge Farm in Mansfield, Missouri. There are also chapters about the boyhood home of Laura's husband, Almanzo Wilder, in Malone, New York, and about his later home in Spring Valley, Minnesota. Each chapter tells how its site was founded, as well as what the site looks like today. There is detailed information on how to get to the sites and where to stay, and on other places of interest to visit in the surrounding countryside, much of which is as rugged and remote as when Laura lived in her little houses.

Laura had been only partially right when she ended *Little House in the Big Woods*: "Now is now. It can never be a long time ago." It is still possible to know the "long time ago" of the Ingalls and Wilder families. Through the pages of the Little House books and the open doors of the places Laura Ingalls Wilder once called home, we can visit Laura's pioneer days and enter, for a time at least, the world of long ago.

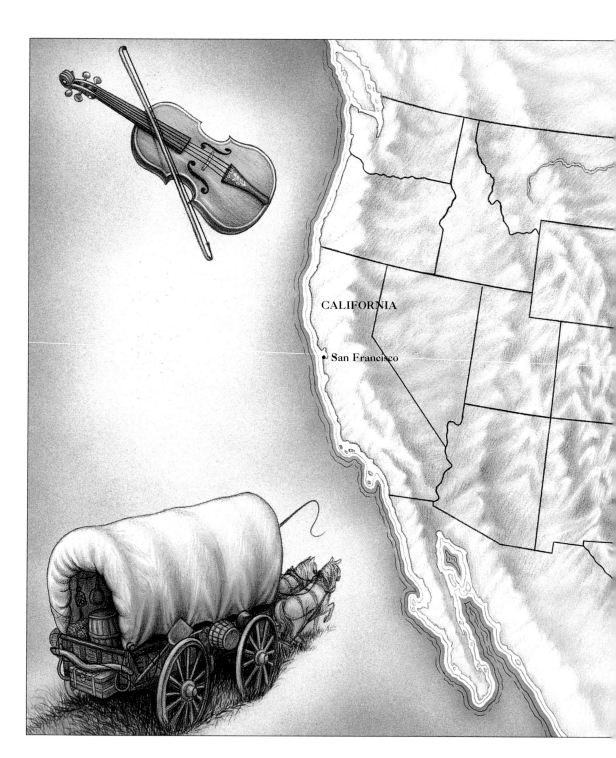

CALIFORNIA

San Francisco

"Once upon a time . . . a little girl lived in the Big Woods
of Wisconsin, in a little gray house made of logs."
—LITTLE HOUSE IN THE BIG WOODS

PEPIN, WISCONSIN, AND THE LITTLE HOUSE IN THE BIG WOODS

LAURA AND THE BIG WOODS

*L*ittle House in the Big Woods, first published in 1932, is where Little House all began. This very first Little House book captivated readers of all ages with the pioneer story of Laura; her Pa and Ma; her big sister, Mary; and her baby sister, Carrie. Soon the Little House books would become household names, and readers would avidly follow the adventures of Laura and her family as they moved farther west into the American frontier. But these adventures all began in Laura's comfortable little log house in the middle of the Big Woods of Wisconsin.

Charles and Caroline Ingalls, Laura's Pa and Ma, were both among the earliest pioneers in western Wisconsin. Laura's mother was born in Brookfield, Wisconsin, in 1839 and may have been the first non-Indian baby born in the area. (Brookfield is now a thickly populated suburb of Milwaukee.) After Caroline and Charles were married, they rented land in the Concord area for a few years. Then they settled on land about seven miles from the river town of Pepin, founded in 1855. Pa built his family a little log cabin. Soon Mary was born in 1865, and then Laura in 1867. The family farmed the land, and Pa traded, shopped and voted in town, and fished in Lake Pepin.

The little house in the Wisconsin woods was the Ingalls home twice. Pa sold his land in 1868, and the following year he took his family to Kansas. The buyer of the land defaulted on his payments, however, and the land reverted to Pa. In 1871, the family

Left: The Little House in the Big Woods replica cabin

returned to the Big Woods to live. They remained there until 1874, when they moved west to Minnesota. This second period of residence is what Laura recalled in *Little House in the Big Woods*.

THE FOUNDING OF THE SITE

The first commemoration of *Little House in the Big Woods* came in 1961–1962, when the local library committee succeeded in locating the land that had been the Ingalls farm. Subsequently, the Pepin village park was named the Laura Ingalls Wilder Park, and a historical marker was placed near the Ingalls cabin site.

Little House in the Big Woods historical marker

Though the original cabin had vanished by the 1920s, a shallow place in the land marking the site of the cabin and some foundation stones were still evident in the thick underbrush.

In 1974, the Laura Ingalls Wilder Memorial Society was founded to develop the cabin site further. Three acres of land were donated by the owners for this purpose. In 1976 and 1977, the "Little House Wayside," as the site came to be known, became a reality. A replica of the cabin, picnic area, well, and historical marker completed the site. Over the years most of the land around the site has been cleared for farming, but trees have

The Big Woods near Pepin

been planted around the Wayside to give it a more authentic feel.

WHAT TO SEE AND DO

The first stop for Little House fans is, of course, the **Little House Wayside** itself. To reach the site, take Country Road CC 7 miles north from Pepin. The winding two-lane road approximates Pa's trail into town; parts of the route are still heavily forested. To truly appreciate the Big Woods, though, turn off any one of the side roads. On these roads, big trees make leafy overheads and evoke Laura's memories of the Wisconsin woods. At the site there is a three-room replica cabin of the one Pa built in 1863. Although the house is unfurnished—since no one lives on the grounds, it would be too easy to vandalize—it is divided into three rooms: a living room with a fireplace, a bedroom, and a pantry, which Laura described in her book.

The replica cabin is located on the grounds of the **Laura Ingalls Wilder Park**. There are picnic tables available for all visitors. Also in the park is the **Pepin Railroad Depot Museum**. The 1886 Burlington depot was

The Pepin Railroad Depot Museum

moved in 1985 from its original locale along Lake Pepin and is now on the edge of the park. The Depot Museum has displays on Mississippi River lore and on the story of early railroading, logging, and boating on the lake. Open daily May 15–Oct. 15, 10 to 5 (telephone during open months: 715-442-2142; off season call 800-442-3011). Admission is by donation.

For more information on the Ingalls family and the Little House in the Big Woods, and on memberships to the local memorial society, contact the Laura Ingalls Wilder Memorial Society, P.O. Box 269, Pepin, WI 54759; tel. 715-442-2248. Always include a stamp with your inquiry.

While the main Little House site of the area is the replica cabin, the Laura Ingalls Wilder connection is proclaimed throughout the town of Pepin by blue banners carrying a log cabin logo. The **Pepin Historical Museum** features exhibits on Laura Ingalls Wilder as well as antiques and area history. There is a fully stocked bookshop with Little House books and related items. The museum is

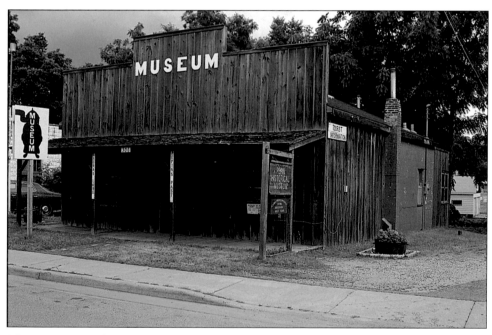

The Pepin Historical Museum

located at 306 Third Street in Pepin. For more information, telephone 715-442-2142 during open months and 715-442-3171 during off season. Open daily May–Oct., 10 to 5. Admission is by donation.

In Pepin's **Oakwood Cemetery**, on the outskirts of town, is the grave of Anna Barry, Laura's first teacher. Also buried in the cemetery is Martha Quiner Carpenter, Caroline's sister and Laura's aunt. Martha was Laura's hostess in 1890, when Laura made her last visit to the Pepin area.

Each September, the **Laura Ingalls Wilder Days Festival** is held. Entertainment includes antiques, a crafts and flea market, a parade, a Laura look-alike pageant, and a play based on *Little House in the Big Woods*. For more information, visit www.pepinwisconsin.com, or contact Laura Ingalls Wilder Days Committee, Box 274, Pepin, WI 54759; tel. 715-442-3011.

Little House fans who wish to pursue other Wisconsin-Ingalls connections can visit several places around Pepin. Laura's grandparents, Lansford and Laura Ingalls, farmed land north of Little House Wayside, near the Pepin and Pierce County line. The site is not marked, and eventually the grandparents moved farther north to Webster. Their graves and those of other family members are in the Orange Cemetery near Webster, about a three-or four-hour drive from Pepin.

About 35 miles west of Milwaukee is an area closely associated with the early lives of Caroline and Charles Ingalls. In 1860, Pa and Ma were married in the little town of **Concord**, and they spent the next three years in the vicinity. To see the thinly populated countryside around Concord, take the Sullivan-Ixonia exit from I-94. Just off Highway F is the tiny village of Concord. Only a few buildings, a park, a town hall, and an elementary school are left. South of Concord, via Highways F and 18, is the town of Rome. In the Rome Cemetery is the grave of Laura's grandmother, Charlotte Quiner Holbrook. Her grave and that of her second husband, Frederick Holbrook, are marked with headstones from the 1880s.

For those Little House fans who wish to explore the immediate area Laura was born in, they need look no farther than **Pepin** itself. Pepin offers such a myriad of experiences for visitors that it can be hard to decide which to do first—enjoy all the sports and activities of the lake; browse among the many antique shops, gift shops, and crafts studios; or dip into the history of the village. The Pepin that Laura once visited was situated on Front Street, on the edge of Lake Pepin. There the original stores and businesses of the 1860s and 1870s clustered. Today, Pepin's waterfront and indeed the whole area enjoys an active tourist business. Two blocks south of Highway 35, Pepin's waterfront offers access to the lake for swimming, boating, fishing, and camping. The **Pepin Marina** has almost 150 slips and docks for those arriving via the Mississippi River. Just west of the marina is the public beach. For more information about the marina, call 715-442-4900.

The Pepin Marina is, of course, at the edge of **Lake Pepin**, on whose

Mississippi River near Pepin

shores Laura and her family picnicked. The lake is a 3-mile widening of the Mississippi, and is 30 miles long. Majestic bluffs, some of them up to 400 feet high, were full of legends and Indian lore, even in Laura's time. Mark Twain, who often praised the Mississippi, extolled Lake Pepin's spectacular views. "It is the true Sunset Land," he wrote. "I am sure no other country can show so good a right to the name." While many years have passed since Twain viewed Lake Pepin, sunsets over the lake remain just as spectacular. Indeed, the entire Pepin area is one of the most beautiful of any of the places Laura lived. Rivers, dense forests, green hills and valleys, and the bluffs of the Mississippi River create a landscape that is both fertile and lush.

A circuit around Lake Pepin known as the **Great River Road** makes a wonderful day trip after visiting the Little House sites. The Wisconsin side of the lake is bordered by Highway 35, which passes through Bay City, Maiden Rock, Stockholm, Pepin, Nelson, and Alma. Bridges at Red Wing and Wabasha link the route to Highway 61 in Minnesota. There are six more towns along the Minnesota shore: Frontenac, Lake City, Camp LaCupolis, Reads Landing, Wabasha, and Kellogg. Each community has its own charm and a variety of attractions, including camping, fishing, boating, and arts-and-crafts shopping. For example, **Stockholm** is a historic village that showcases the work of local and international artisans in its many village shops and galleries. There is even an annual **Stockholm Art Fair** on the third Saturday in July. **Maiden Rock**, so named for the Indian princess who jumped off the bluff rather than marry a man she did not

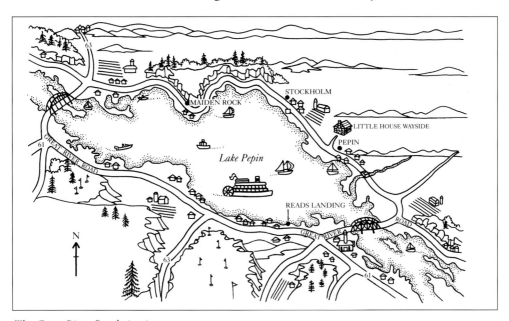

The Great River Road circuit

Lake Pepin

love, boasts a 25-mile-wide panoramic view of Lake Pepin's bluffs and a lake-side campground. The **Wabasha County Historical Society Museum** at Reads Landing hosts an Ingalls family exhibit, among other period displays. The museum is located on Second Street, off Highway 61, in an 1870 school building. Open daily mid-May–mid-Oct., 12 to 4, or by appointment. Tel. 877-525-3248 for Lake City Tourism or 651-345-2692, or e-mail mberoos@yahoo.com.

For more information and a map of Lake Pepin and "The Dozen Vintage Villages," visit www.pepinwisconsin.com or contact Pepin Information Center, Box 161, Pepin, WI 54759; tel. 715-442-3011.

WHERE TO EAT AND STAY

Many restaurants line the streets of Pepin, including **The Harbor View Cafe** (314 First Street; tel. 715-442-3893; www.harborviewpepin.com), which offers homemade gourmet dining. Open

Maiden Rock

mid-March–mid-Nov., Thurs.–Mon. **The Pickle Factory** (105 First Street; tel. 715-442-4400; www.pepinpickle-factory.com) is open for lunch and dinner and serves hamburgers and other cafe food. **Ralph's Bar/Mary's Kitchen** (206 Lake Street; tel. 715-442-3451) specializes in burgers and is open daily, all year round, for breakfast, lunch, and dinner.

A variety of bed-and-breakfasts are located in the Pepin area. A current list can be obtained from the Pepin Visitor's Information Center, tel. 800-442-3011; e-mail info@pepin-wisconsin.com, or visit www.pepin-wisconsin.com. There is also a large campground facility a half block away from Highway 35 called the **Bumble Bee Inn and Campground** (200 Washington Street; tel. 715-442-2592). Open Apr.-Nov.

For a unique eating and lodging alternative, travelers may enjoy **The Anderson House** across the lake in Wabasha. The hotel, established in 1856, is Minnesota's oldest operating inn. Bountiful meals of home cooking are served in the dining room; guest rooms are furnished with antiques. An unexpected amenity is the availability of resident cats, which are assigned to guests on request. For information, write or call The Anderson House, 333 W. Main Street, Wabasha, MN 55981; tel. 651-565-4524; www.historicandersonhouse.com.

HOW TO GET THERE

I-90 is a major east-west route south of Pepin. At La Crosse, travelers can take Highway 35, also known as the Great River Road, north to Lake Pepin. From Minneapolis-St. Paul to the north, Pepin is less than a ninety-minute drive.

The closest Little House sites to Pepin are Burr Oak, Iowa, and Spring Valley, Minnesota, approximately two to two and a half hours away. Walnut Grove, Minnesota, is about 370 miles west; and De Smet, South Dakota, is about 470 miles west. Mansfield, Missouri, is about 665 miles south.

"As far as they could see, to the east and to the south and to the west, nothing was moving on all the vastness of the High Prairie. Only the green grass was rippling in the wind, and white clouds drifted in the high, clear sky."
—LITTLE HOUSE ON THE PRAIRIE

INDEPENDENCE, KANSAS, AND THE LITTLE HOUSE ON THE PRAIRIE

LAURA AND THE PRAIRIE

*L*ittle House on the Prairie recounts the Ingalls family's first journey to the western prairies. The Big Woods had become too crowded, so Pa and Ma traveled west by covered wagon with their girls and their trusty bulldog, Jack. No one knows the route they followed, but the journey across Minnesota, Iowa, Missouri, and Kansas would have taken several months. (Nowadays, the trip would take approximately two days by car.) When they arrived in the southeastern corner of Kansas, Pa looked around and liked the wide open prairie land. So the Ingalls family settled down to start a new life in what is now part of Montgomery County, Kansas.

What Pa did not know was that the family had settled on land called the Osage Diminished Reserve. This was an area that the government had set aside for the Osage Indians, and it included most of Montgomery County. While the Indians were away on one of their periodic hunting trips farther west, settlers arrived and, thinking the land was available, began building homesteads. The Ingalls family was among these settlers. Until Congress passed an act to buy the Reserve from the Osage tribes at a fair price, there was unrest between the tribes and the pioneers. Laura described this unrest in *Little House on the Prairie*.

While Pa never officially filed for a homestead, the family was included in the 1870 census of the area. Pa, Ma, Mary, Laura, and baby Carrie were listed as the eighty-ninth household in Rutland Township.

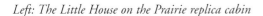

Left: The Little House on the Prairie replica cabin

THE FOUNDING OF THE SITE

Pa's hand-dug well

Ever since *Little House on the Prairie* was first published in 1935, readers have wondered where the little house actually stood. They knew from the book that Independence was the nearest town, but where on the vast prairie was the house?

Margaret Clement, a local bookseller, and Eilene Charbo of the Kansas State Historical Society did research that finally pinpointed the cabin site on property owned by Wilma and Bill Kurtis of Independence. With help from local organizations in Independence, a log cabin replica was eventually erected on the site. It was dedicated in 1977. Nearby rocks were unearthed that suggested a foundation for the original cabin or the stable. Next to the foundation, a hand-dug well was discovered. It is in excellent condition and is undoubtedly the well Pa dug with a neighbor's help. A small-sized horseshoe was found under layers of earth—just the size to fit Pet or Patty, the Ingallses' mustangs.

The Kurtis family—Wilma; her husband, Brigadier General William

Front view of the Little House on the Prairie cabin

The inside of the Little House on the Prairie

Kurtis, USMC Retired; and their son, distinguished network news anchor and documentary host Bill Kurtis—agreed that the Little House site should remain simple and uncluttered so that visitors can experience that same feeling of the open prairie that the Ingallses knew so well.

WHAT TO SEE AND DO

The **Little House on the Prairie** sits among miles of flat open prairie land. Just as when Laura lived on the prairie, the wind gently blows, the grasses wave, and the sounds of birds and insects are harmonious and lovely. The one-room replica cabin is furnished exactly as Laura described in *Little House on the Prairie*. Open March–Oct., Mon.–Sat., 10 to 5; Sun., 1 to 5. Admission is by donation. For more information about the Little House on the Prairie, write Little House on the Prairie Inc., Box 110, Independence, KS 67301; tel: 620-289-4238; www.littlehouseontheprairie.com. Always include a stamp with your inquiry.

Near the cabin replica are two authentic buildings from Laura's era.

The one-room schoolhouse

One is the tiny, turn-of-the-century **post office**, which once served nearby Wayside, Kansas. Visitors may purchase postcards of the cabin, as well as other souvenirs and the Little House books. Close by is **Sunnyside School**, built in 1872 and used until 1947. This one-room school is furnished with desks from the 1870s and 1880s, and other authentic country school details, including a framed portrait of Lincoln. When the Little House on the Prairie site was developed, the Sunnyside School was moved to the site from its original location a few miles distant.

Nearby is **Independence**, the town where Pa bought Ma sugar and eight squares of window glass, which was established in 1870. It is a quintessential prairie town, with wide tree-lined streets and a population of about 9,500. Many of the businesses

Dr. Tann's grave

Edmund Mason's (Mr. Edwards's) grave

and buildings along its main street, Penn Avenue, date back to the pioneers who first settled the town. Buried in the local **Mount Hope Cemetery** is one Little House–related pioneer—Dr. George Tann (1825–1909). Dr. Tann was the doctor to the Osage who also cared for the Ingalls family during a malaria epidemic. (Laura spelled his name "Tan" in *Little House on the Prairie*.) The cemetery is located on Highway 75 North in Independence. There is an entrance on Catalpa Street. Buried in **Harrison Cemetery** is Edmund Mason (1846–1906), who is believed to have been Mr. Edwards, the Ingallses' kind bachelor neighbor.

Independence is also the home-town of two twentieth-century personalities. Vivian Vance, who played Ethel Mertz in the long-running *I Love Lucy* show, was a native. So was William Inge, the Academy Award– and Pulitzer Prize–winning playwright of *Splendor in the Grass* and *Picnic*. A collection of Inge's memorabilia is at **The Independence Community College**, which also holds an annual Inge Festival in late April. For more information, call 316-331-4100, ext. 4275.

The Independence Historical Museum is one of the city's prime cultural attractions. Over twenty rooms of American, Asian and European antiques and art are on exhibit in this museum; each room focuses on a particular culture or theme (120 N. Eighth Street; tel. 316-331-3515; www.kansastravel.org/independence-museum.htm). Open Wed.–Sat., 10 to 4. Admission: $3, children under 12 free.

Nearby, at **The Science and Technology Center** (125 S. Penn Ave.; tel. 316-331-1999), visitors can have a completely contemporary and

The prairie near Independence

hands-on experience with such things as an anti-gravity simulator and the hair-raising Van de Graaff generator. Open daily, 1 to 5. Admission: $3.

Every year in the last full week in October, Independence hosts **Neewollah** (*Halloween* spelled backward). This celebration, which was first held in 1919, features musical stage shows, carnivals, street acts, arts and crafts, and various entertainers. It is topped off with a two-hour parade through Independence. For more information, contact Neewollah, Inc., P.O. Box 311, Independence, KS 67301, or visit its website at www.neewollah.com.

The Riverside Park/Ralph Mitchell Zoo is a 124-acre park, which boasts a nickel merry-go-round and a miniature train you can ride. There is also a miniature golf course on the grounds. The zoo hosts bears, monkeys, buffalo, cougars, an elephant, an aviary, a swan pond, and a flock of tame peacocks that roam about at will. Check the park's website, www.forpaz.com/home.htm, for park hours. Admission is free. For more information about Independence in general, contact the Independence Convention and Visitor's Bureau, 322 N. Penn Avenue, Independence, KS 63701; tel. 316-331-1890 or 800-882-3606, or visit www.indks.chamber.org.

Elk City Lake, 5 miles northwest of Independence, offers a wide variety of outdoor recreation and features a shoreline nearly 50 miles in length. You can hunt, fish, camp, boat, swim, hike, and picnic on and around the lake, and there are several marked and well-maintained hiking trails. Open all year. For more information contact Elk City State Park, P.O. Box 945, Independence, KS 63701; tel. 316-331-6295.

WHERE TO EAT AND STAY

Independence has over a dozen restaurants and fast-food establishments. Among them are **Woods** (120 W. Laurel; tel. 316-331-7960), a family restaurant serving lunch and dinner; **Sirloin Stockade** (2125 N. Penn; tel. 316-331-1777), specializing in home cooking and beef entrees; and **Cowboy Café** (1921 W. Main; tel. 316-331-2141), which is open for breakfast, lunch, and dinner, and offers buffet specials. There are also many Mexican and Chinese restaurants in the Independence area.

Among Independence's many motels are **Appletree Inn** (201 N. Eighth Street, tel. 316-331-5500); **Townsman Motel** (1112 E. Main, tel. 316-331-5400); **Hillcrest Inn** (3146 N. Penn Ave., tel. 316-331-5750); **Lamplighter Inn** (2320 W. Main, tel. 316-331-4655); **Rosewood Bed and Breakfast** (417 W. Myrtle, tel. 316-331-2221). The city address for all is Independence, KS 67301.

HOW TO GET THERE

The Little House on the Prairie is located 13 miles southwest of Independence, just off Highway 75. Follow green-and-white historical markers. Independence itself is located at the junction of Highways 160 and 75 in southeastern Kansas near the Kansas-Oklahoma border. The closest cities to the site are Tulsa, Oklahoma, about 90 miles away; Wichita, Kansas, about 125 miles away; and Kansas City, Missouri, about 180 miles away. The closest airport is 90 miles away, in Tulsa. The closest Little House site is Mansfield, Missouri, about five to six hours away by car.

LAURA'S DUGOUT HOME
ON THE BANKS OF PLUM CREEK

THE CHARLES INGALLS FAMILY'S DUGOUT HOME
WAS LOCATED HERE IN THE 1870s. THIS DEPRESSION
IS ALL THAT REMAINS SINCE THE ROOF CAVED IN
YEARS AGO. THE PRAIRIE GRASSES AND FLOWERS
HERE GROW MUCH AS THEY DID IN LAURA'S TIME,
AND THE SPRING STILL FLOWS NEARBY.

"Laura could see a creek. She saw a grassy bank, and beyond it a line of willow tree tops, waving in the gentle wind. Everywhere else the prairie grasses were rippling far away to the sky's straight edge."
—ON THE BANKS OF PLUM CREEK

WALNUT GROVE, MINNESOTA, AND THE BANKS OF PLUM CREEK

LAURA AND WALNUT GROVE

Only a year after they moved to the prairie, the Ingalls family discovered their land belonged to the Osage. So they packed up their covered wagon once again and drove across southern Minnesota, seeking a new home in the west. They stopped along the banks of Plum Creek, near the frontier village of Walnut Grove. Through the winter months they lived in a sod dugout—a one-room house literally carved out of the banks of Plum Creek. Then Pa built a two-story frame house nearby. Laura called this house, the largest she had ever lived in, "the wonderful house." Today the Ingallses' route to Plum Creek and their dugout homesite are among Minnesota's most famous historical attractions.

Ironically, Laura never actually mentioned Walnut Grove in her book *On the Banks of Plum Creek*. In fact, it was not until 1947, when Garth Williams arrived in town to sketch sites for the reillustration of the Little House books, that local residents learned that their Plum Creek was the one Laura used in her title and that Walnut Grove was the town Laura described in the book.

THE FOUNDING OF THE SITE

During the 1950s and 1960s Little House fans sought out the physical traces of the Ingallses' years by Plum Creek. Beginning their quest at the offices of *The Walnut Grove Tribune*, many were then directed to the Gordon family farm, which was on land that had once

Left: The dugout site on the banks of Plum Creek

been the Ingalls homestead. There the gracious Gordons showed visitors the creek, dugout site, and other memorable spots mentioned in Laura's story.

The debut of the television series *Little House on the Prairie* in 1974 did mention Walnut Grove by name—seven times in the first show. That national exposure brought such a flood of visitors to the area that a Laura Ingalls Wilder Committee was formed, and a Visitor's Center and Museum were established. The quiet acres of the Gordon farm were soon transformed into a thriving tourist destination, accessible to cars, campers, and bus tours filled with Little House fans eager to see and explore the land where Laura, Pa, Ma, Mary, and Carrie once lived.

In 1994, over one hundred years after the Ingalls family followed a covered-wagon trail to their new homestead, the route they took to Plum Creek was designated the Laura Ingalls Wilder Historic Highway. Every dozen or so miles, from Mankato, Minnesota, to Lake Benton, Minnesota, near the South Dakota border, green-and-white signs bearing Laura's name mark the way. They are placed along U.S. Highway 14, a pleasant, nearly straight road that passes cornfields and farmhouses and seven heartland towns on the way to Walnut Grove.

WHAT TO SEE AND DO

The most important site in Walnut Grove is, of course, the former **Ingalls farm** on the banks of Plum Creek. Travel 1.5 miles north of Walnut Grove on Country Road 5. Signs beckon travelers to drive into the farmyard where a red barn and frame house stand. The "wonderful house" Laura described has vanished, although the Gordons have several ideas about where the frame house might have stood. However, the land is much the same as in Laura's day, with tall prairie grass and few trees, and you can see the dugout site.

Plum Creek flows through thickets of trees. You can cross the creek by

Plum Creek

a footbridge; on the other side, a winding path leads to a hollow in the ground where the sod dugout once stood. A marker stands on the site of the dugout. Local old-timers say the grass roof caved in during the 1920s and the walls melted into the prairie sod, but the surrounding land is exactly as Laura described it. There are still wild plum trees growing, and the nearby spring still flows. Peaceful and mostly untouched, this is perhaps the most unchanged of all the book locales. The dugout site is open until sunset on every day that has good weather. Admission is $4 per car and $20 per tour bus.

Another beautiful spot nearby is the **Plum Creek Park**. This area was once the original walnut grove that

Downtown Walnut Grove

gave the town its name back in the 1870s. Now Lake Laura and Plum Creek, both in the park, offer spots for hikes, swimming, and fishing. A campground has forty wooded and electrified sites.

Walnut Grove is a typical Mid-western small town, with straight, symmetrical streets, a water tower, and tidy businesses along the main street. The site of the first school in town, attended by Laura and Mary and Nellie Oleson, is at Fourth and Washington. And, although the Reverend Alden's Congregational Church was torn down in 1954, the church bell that Pa helped to buy still rings in the belfry of the English Lutheran church.

Church bell that Pa helped to buy

The Laura Ingalls Wilder Museum

The **Laura Ingalls Wilder Museum** is at 330 Eighth Street, just off Highway 14. The complex of buildings includes an 1898 depot containing pioneer and railroad exhibits, a bookstore, a tiny "chapel," a schoolhouse, and exhibits on the town's history. "Grandma's House," an onion-domed 1890s house, has period rooms and the Kelton Doll Collection, featuring 250 dolls from the 1870s to the present day.

Admission is free for children 5 and under, $2 for children 6–12, and $5 for anyone 13 and over. Please contact the Museum for hours. For more information about the Laura Ingalls Wilder Museum and Tourist Information Center and the town of Walnut Grove, contact 330 8th St., Walnut Grove, MN 56180; tel. 800-528-7280. Always enclose a stamp with your inquiry. For more information on any of the sites, visit www.walnutgrove.org.

Walnut Grove takes its Little House connections very seriously. Every summer since 1978, Walnut Grove residents don costumes of the 1870s to present a two-act pageant about the

Scene from the annual "Fragments of a Dream" pageant

Ingalls family and their friends called **"Fragments of a Dream."** Authentic sets, live animals, special effects, and the natural amphitheater along Plum Creek make this play a perfect representation of Walnut Grove's pioneer history. For tickets, call 800-859-3102. The prairie just west of town comes alive with this presentation every summer for the first three weekends in July. There is also a **Walnut Grove Family Festival** held the second and third weekends in July. During the daytime on the pageant grounds, there are craft demonstrations, live music, children's activities, as well as souvenirs and crafts for sale. For more information about the two festivals, exact dates, and prices, contact Wilder Pageant Committee, P.O. Box 313, 11505 Crown Ave., Walnut Grove, MN 56180; tel. 507-859-2174 or 888-859-3102.

Seven miles west of Walnut Grove is **Tracy**. Tracy is the town where Ma and the Ingalls girls disembarked from their first train ride. The **Wheels Across the Prairie Museum** (tel. 507-629-3661) on W. Highway 14 in Tracy focuses on early pioneer transportation. Open 1 to 5 every day from Memorial Day through September 15, and by request. Suggested donation is $2 for adults, children free.

Prairie schooner outside the Laura Ingalls Wilder Museum

burgers, sandwiches, and other home-style meals. In nearby Tracy you will find the **Red Rooster Restaurant** (Highway 14; tel. 507-629-9959), similar to Nellie's Café.

There are no lodgings in Walnut Grove. The nearest lodging is in Tracy, at **Wilder Inn** (1000 Craig Ave., Tracy, MN 56175; tel. 507-629-3350). Ten minutes east of Walnut Grove is the **Lamberton Motel** (601 First Ave. W., Lamberton, MN 56152; tel. 507-752-7242). Other attractions and accommodations in southwest Minnesota are listed in brochures available from Redwood Regional Tourism, Box 21, Redwood Falls, MN 56283; tel. 507-637-2828 or 800-657-7070.

WHERE TO EAT AND STAY

Walnut Grove has one restaurant in town, **Nellie's Café** (Highway 14; tel. 507-859-2384). It is open seven days a week: Mon.–Fri. from 6 A.M. to 4 P.M., Sat. from 6 A.M. to 2 P.M., and Sun. from 6 A.M. to 1 P.M. Nellie's Cafe also has extended hours during Pageant Week. It serves

HOW TO GET THERE

Walnut Grove is about 150 miles from the Twin Cities, on Highway 14, the Laura Ingalls Wilder Historic Highway. A few hours farther west on the same road is De Smet, South Dakota.

BURR OAK, IOWA

LAURA AND THE MASTERS HOTEL

In 1876, the Ingalls family left Walnut Grove as refugees from the grasshopper invasion that plagued a wide swath of Minnesota. As "back-trailers" (pioneers who traveled first west, then east), they headed east, and settled for a while in Wabasha County, Minnesota, where they lived with Peter Ingalls, Pa's brother, and his family.

Peter never owned his land near the Zumbro River, so pinpointing that little house has been impossible. While Pa and Ma and their family lived there, their only son, Charles Frederic, died. His grave site has never been found despite a painstaking search. The family Bible records his death at South Troy, Minnesota. A present-day road sign marked "South Troy" is found along Highway 63, with a church nearby. Some seekers have assumed that the baby's grave must be in the church cemetery, but this is not true. During the 1870s, South Troy was farther north and east. It is unlikely that the grave will ever be discovered.

From Minnesota, the Ingallses moved next to Burr Oak, Iowa, and lived there from 1876 to 1878. There the family helped to run the Burr Oak Masters Hotel.

Laura never wrote of this part of her childhood in her Little House books. In 2002, Newbery Medal–winning author Cynthia Rylant wrote *Old Town in the Green Groves*, which was based on Laura's unpublished memoirs about her time in Burr Oak. Laura's life in Burr Oak resulted in the Laura Ingalls Wilder Park and Museum,

Left: The restored Masters Hotel

unique among the Little House sites.

THE FOUNDING OF THE SITE

Rumors that Burr Oak was a stopping place for the Ingalls family began surfacing during the 1930s with Rose Wilder Lane's mention of the town in a magazine short story and Laura's mounting fame as a writer. Rose drove through the town in the 1930s, seeking and finding people who remembered her family. Laura substantiated the stories that she had lived there in an article in the 1940s in the *Decorah Public Opinion*, a nearby newspaper.

It was not until the 1970s, though, that a group was formed to find the former Ingalls home. A search of the town property records revealed that the actual eleven-room frontier hotel was still standing—albeit in a state of disrepair. The four founders of the future Laura Ingalls Wilder Park and Museum acquired the property and set out to restore it,

with the help of a series of benefits and a penny drive by local schoolchildren. The grounds were also developed for recreation and picnicking. In 1976, the site began to offer organized tours.

WHAT TO SEE AND DO

Today Burr Oak is a quiet little town, whose population hovers around 100. A scattering of homes, a church, and a general store are the backdrop for the **Laura Ingalls Wilder Museum**, formerly known as the Burr Oak Masters Hotel. During its heyday Burr Oak was a crossroads for pioneers heading west; as many as two hundred covered wagons sometimes stopped there for the night. Now the tiny rooms in the restored eleven-room building are filled with antiques, period clothing, and artifacts; and tour guides recount the role of the pioneer hotel and the Ingalls family's connection to it.

The main floor of the hotel consists of the barroom that Pa and Ma hated, the hotel parlor, and a guest

Courtesy of William Anderson

The old Masters Hotel

room. The parlor includes an 1880s pump organ and other period pieces. Behind the parlor is the guest room presumed to have been used by the star boarder, Mr. Bisbee. Wealthy Mr. Bisbee attempted to teach ten-year-old Laura Ingalls musical scales on the organ.

A central stairway leads to tiny, cubiclelike sleeping rooms upstairs. A lower-level basement area served as the kitchen and dining area, where Laura and Mary helped Ma and Pa by waiting on tables. Authentic utensils, dishes, and a wood range are on display.

The museum is open year-round with varying hours of operation. Visit its website, www.lauraingalls-wilder.us, or call 563-735-5916 for more information. Admission: $5 for adults, $4 for seniors (over 60), $3 for children 6–17; free for children 5 and under. A family pass is available for $12. For more information, contact Laura Ingalls Wilder Park and Museum, 3603 236th Ave., Burr Oak, IA 52101. Always include a stamp with your inquiry.

Next door to the Wilder Park and Museum is an unexpected treat, the **Burr Oak Mercantile Store**. The almost century-old general store (the original structure burned down) still

retains the aura of pioneer days. The original mahogany woodwork gleams behind the items for sale—groceries, sundries, local craft items, and souvenirs. It also serves lunches, light snacks, and homemade pies. The **Burr Oak Post Office**, where postcards can be stamped and canceled with the town's name, occupies a cubbyhole in the store.

Winneshiek County, where Burr Oak is located, is a quintessential peaceful farming area, with gentle wooded hills, limestone bluffs, and flowing streams. Biking and canoeing are popular because of the scenic views.

Decorah, about 10 miles south of Burr Oak, has a decidedly Norwegian flavor. **The Vesterheim**, a Norwegian-American museum in a complex of fourteen buildings, recounts the immigration experience of Scandinavians. In addition to the museum, a gift shop and cafe are located at the headquarters on 523 W. Water Street, Decorah, IA 52101; tel. 563-382-9681; http://vesterheim.org/index.php.

The museum is open daily May–Oct., 9 to 5, and Tues.–Sun., Nov.–Apr., 10 to 4. Admission ranges from free to $5, depending on age and season of year. Group and family discounts available.

The Masters Hotel today

About 12 miles southwest of Decorah is **Spillville**, a village with a Czechoslovakian atmosphere. Czech composer Antonín Dvořák had a summer house in Spillville, which is now a museum. Museum exhibits include Dvořák memorabilia and an exhibit of handmade musical clocks, some over seven feet tall. For more information about Decorah, Spillville, and Winneshiek County, call 800-463-4692 or 563-382-3990, or visit www.decorah-iowa.com.

WHERE TO EAT AND STAY

Burr Oak Mercantile Store (tel. 563-735-5500) is open from 11 A.M. to 10 P.M. It serves breakfast, lunch, and dinner and specializes in homemade pie and gourmet pizza. Next door to the museum is **Bruskie's Bar and Grill** (tel. 563-735-5550), which is open 10 A.M. to 10 P.M. Mon.–Sat., and 12 P.M. to 8 P.M. on Sun. and serves lunch and dinner. Picnic facilities and a playground are behind the museum where Silver Creek angles through the property.

There are no lodgings in Burr Oak, but 3 miles away in Decorah are two motels: **Heartland Inn** (705 Commerce Drive; tel. 800-334-3277, ext. 24 or 563-382-2269; www.heartlandinns.com); and **Decorah Super 8** (810 Highway 9E, Box 465; tel. 800-800-8000 or 563-382-8771; www.super8.com). The city address for all is Decorah, IA 52101. For a complete listing of all of the facilities in the general area, call 800-463-4692 or 563-382-3990, or visit the Decorah website at www.decorah-iowa.com.

HOW TO GET THERE

Burr Oak is located in extreme northeastern Iowa, 3 miles from the Minnesota border. The town is just off Highway 52. Pepin, Wisconsin, is about two hours north, and Spring Valley, Minnesota, is about a forty-five-minute drive.

"The town was so changed that it seemed like a new place. Two whole blocks on the west side of Main Street were solidly filled with new, yellow-pine buildings. A new board sidewalk was in front of them."
—LITTLE TOWN ON THE PRAIRIE

DE SMET, SOUTH DAKOTA, AND THE LITTLE TOWN ON THE PRAIRIE

LAURA AND THE LITTLE TOWN ON THE PRAIRIE

In 1879, the Ingalls family moved again, this time to follow Pa's job with the Winona–St. Peter Railway. The railroad was being extended west from Tracy, Minnesota, to Huron, Dakota Territory. (Not until 1889 did the territory split into North and South Dakota.) Although railroad construction stopped during the winter of 1879–1880, Pa Ingalls and his family remained in the Surveyor's House, as Laura wrote in *By the Shores of Silver Lake*. They were the only settlers for miles around, and in fact, they were officially made the first settlers of De Smet when it was established in 1880.

De Smet was the family's last stop on their long trek west. Despite the harsh and bitter winter Laura described in *The Long Winter*, during which the Ingalls family and the eighty other settlers almost starved to death, Pa and Ma did not move again. They claimed a homestead east of De Smet and Pa also built a house in town. As De Smet grew, the Ingalls family took an active part in the church, school, and social life, as Laura related in *Little Town on the Prairie*. Pa, after his long pioneering life, became very involved with the community, offering his skills both as the town carpenter and in local government. He even served as De Smet's first justice of the peace.

Laura finished school, and met and married Almanzo Wilder in De Smet. After they married, Laura moved to Almanzo's claim, a few miles away from her parents' claim. Laura wrote about these years in her last two Little House books, *These Happy Golden Years* and *The First Four Years*.

Left: The Ingalls home in De Smet

Although Laura, Almanzo, and their daughter, Rose, left De Smet in 1894, the rest of the Ingalls family stayed in or near the area. Pa built a house on Third Street, and died there in 1902; Ma died in 1924; and Mary, who lived with her parents after she graduated from the Iowa Braille and Sight Saving School (called the Iowa College for the Blind in the Little House books) in Vinton, Iowa (see page 95), died in Keystone in 1928. Carrie lived at home until 1912, when she married and settled in the Black Hills. Grace moved to nearby Manchester in 1901, when she married a farmer.

THE FOUNDING OF THE SITE

The beginning of De Smet as a literary landmark town started in *The De Smet News* office where Carrie had worked for many years. Aubrey Sherwood, the editor and publisher of the newspaper, recognized the importance of De Smet as the setting for Rose's own two books, *Let the Hurricane Roar* and *Free Land*, and for the later Little House books. When each of Laura's Little House books based in De Smet was published, *The De Smet News* reported with pride its publication. Laura appreciated Aubrey Sherwood's interest, and sometimes even asked him to verify the facts she incorporated into her books.

The first inkling that De Smet was destined to become a tourist spot came in the 1940s and 1950s, when book readers began to arrive seeking the sites they knew from Laura's stories. *The De Smet News* became the

Railroad tracks near De Smet

first place to go for information. An inveterate collector of historical materials, Aubrey Sherwood would often delight these "Wilder visitors," as he called them, with a letter he had received from Laura or with some other relic from her past.

In 1957, Mr. Sherwood and other locals founded the Laura Ingalls Wilder Memorial Society. Their first goal was to place a monument on a corner of the Ingalls homestead near town. The landowners donated a tract of the prairie ground, local schoolchildren raised money for the monument, and the first official memorial was completed.

Ten years later, the town celebrated Laura's centennial year by acquiring another site: the Surveyors' House, home of the Ingalls family in *By the Shores of Silver Lake*. The first tours were offered in 1968, after the house had been restored. In 1972, the Ingallses' last home, the house Pa built on Third Street, was purchased. The Memorial Society restored and opened this house, making the family's first and last

Father De Smet

existing houses in De Smet available for tourists.

No one knows exactly why the town became known as De Smet. Its namesake was a Jesuit priest, Father Pierre Jean De Smet, who came from his native Belgium to minister to the Sioux Indians in the Upper Missouri River Valley and the Rocky Mountains. However, Father De Smet was never known to have visited the future De Smet area. Other tag lines in the town's history have labeled it "Cream City" and "The Heart of the Pheasant Paradise." But since mid-century, thanks to Aubrey Sherwood's efforts, it seems that De Smet will be known

The Surveyors' House storage room, with original surveying tools

forever as Laura Ingalls Wilder's "little town on the prairie."

WHAT TO SEE AND DO

De Smet and the surrounding countryside are so full of Ingalls-Wilder associations that to see the sites thoroughly takes at least a full day, if not several days. Tours begin at the **Memorial Society Headquarters**, at the corner of Olivet Avenue and First Street. A Victorian era home contains the gift shop, where maps and information are available. The society provides detailed maps that are included in the price of admission to all the De Smet–Little

House locales. The map in this book on page 49 is similar to the society's map; the numbers on the map correspond to the locations of the various sites described below.

The first stop on the tour is the **Surveyors' House** (1), which is located on the grounds of the Society Headquarters. The Surveyors' House is the oldest building in De Smet, dating back to the 1879 railroad camp. The Ingallses lived there for five months and ran what in essence was a hotel for arriving settlers during the spring of 1880, before moving to a homestead. During the 1880s the building was moved from its Silver Lake locale to the present spot.

Guided tours through the tiny house take visitors through the pantry, main room, bedroom, lean-to, and an upstairs loft. The rooms contain a mixture of authentic and replica furniture. In one corner is a replica of the what-not Pa and Laura crafted; other period furniture fits in with Laura's descriptions from the book. The chest of drawers in the main room is the original chest built by Pa. Many details bring book memories flooding back to readers: the red-checked cloth on the table in the main room, the stocked pantry, the two-doored cookstove that so impressed Laura, and the narrow stair into the sleeping loft.

From the Surveyors' House, visitors

Chest of drawers made by Pa

can cross the street to view the **Discover Laura Center** (2), formerly known as the Sigurd Anderson School, a restored one-room country schoolhouse similar to the schools in which Laura taught. It was originally designated as a tribute to the one-time South Dakota governor who

Main room in the Surveyors' House

taught in this school in 1926–1927. Now visitors can treadle an old sewing machine, spin wool, and learn braille.

The walking or driving tour next proceeds down First Street, past the Kingsbury County Courthouse, a stately 1898 building set in a shady park. At the corner of First and Main are two stops worth making, the **Hazel L. Meyer Memorial Library** (3) and the **De Smet Depot Museum** (4). The library contains a showcase with several Ingalls relics. Original paintings by local artist Harvey Dunn (see also pages 54–55) adorn the walls. The Depot, which replaced the original one that burned in 1905, is now a showplace for wildlife displays and local history. A country print shop contains early printing equipment from *The De Smet News* and a tribute to editor Aubrey Sherwood (1894–1987). Open Memorial Day through Labor Day, Mon.–Sat., 10 to 5. Open all seven days during Pageant weekends. Tel. 605-854-3991 during open season. Free admission.

Behind the library and beside the depot is the **Harvey Dunn School**. Area residents rescued Dunn's childhood school, moved it to town, and restored it. The school contains a tribute to Dunn and showcases his paintings. Free admission.

From the Library and Depot

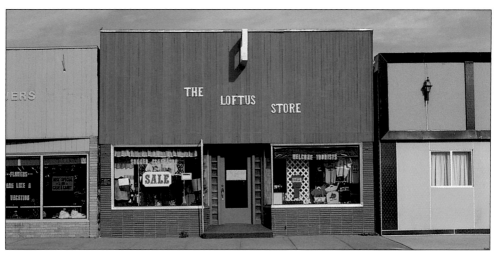

The Loftus Store

Museum, Main Street stretches out in two long blocks. Its store buildings have a decidedly antique look, and many sites will be familiar to Little House readers. There is the **Mead Hotel** site (5), the **Wilder Feed Store** site (6), and the **Fuller Store** site (7). Pa's store building at the corner of Main and Second Streets was moved from its original site after it was sold in 1885 and finally dismantled. The red-brick building (8) now on

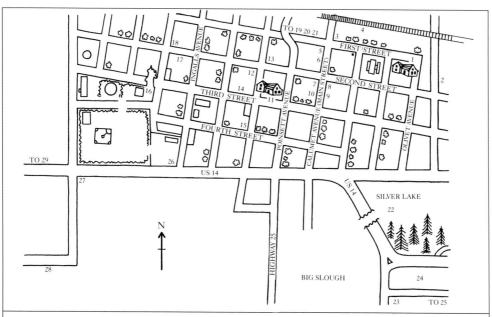

1. The Surveyors' House
2. Discover Laura Center
3. Hazel L. Meyer Memorial Library
4. The De Smet Depot Museum
5. Mead Hotel
6. Wilder Feed Store site
7. Fuller Store site
8. Pa's store site
9. The De Smet News *office*
10. Loftus Store
11. The Ingalls Home
12. The Christian Missionary Alliance Church
13. Original site of the First School
14. Second site of the First School
15. Site of Laura and Almanzo's first house
16. Washington Park
17. The Loftus House
18. Site of the Boast Home
19. The Wilder Homestead
20. Site of Laura and Almanzo's Tree Claim
21. Spirit Lake
23. The Ingalls Homestead Site
24. Laura Ingalls Wilder Pageant grounds
25. The Twin Lakes
26. The Laura Ingalls Wilder Elementary School
27. The Congregational Church
28. De Smet Cemetery

the site is marked with a plaque commemorating Pa's store. *The De Smet News* office (9) comes next, and across the street is the **Loftus Store** (10), still in operation with some of the original fixtures in use. Mr. Loftus sold the wheat that Almanzo and Cap Garland risked their lives for in *The Long Winter*.

From Main Street, the tour proceeds to Third Street and the original residential part of town. East-west streets are numbered; north-south avenues are now designated with historical names. The most important site in this neighborhood is the **Ingalls Home** (11) on Third, between Poinsett and Loftus. The comfortable

The kitchen

gray frame home that housed the Ingalls family from 1887 to 1928 has been restored and is a place to linger and look.

The house was originally built in two sections. The first section was a two-room house on what is now the east side of the house. Later, Pa added on a larger four-room addition of a parlor and three bedrooms. A low kitchen wing is at the back.

The house suggests a much more comfortable life for the Ingallses than any of their previous little houses, probably because they stayed in it for so many years. It has wallpaper, lace curtains, a fancy nickel heater, and comfortable furnishings; it is a palace compared with their earlier shanties and cabins.

There are tour guides at the Ingalls home to help interpret the house. Downstairs are the dining room; the parlor; the kitchen, which is a display area for many of the Ingallses' original possessions; Ma and Pa's bedroom; and Mary's bedroom. The cupboard Pa built dominates one end of the kitchen. The narrow, twisting stairway

The Ingallses' parlor

is the original, but it is too weak to use; access to the second floor is via an outside stair at the back of the house, which was present during the Ingallses' times. There are three more bedrooms upstairs. One showcases Grace's belongings, one displays Carrie's, and the last includes some of Rose's belongings, including her massive writing desk.

From the Ingalls home, another walking opportunity leads the visitor around the corner to the current **Christian Missionary Alliance Church** (12). The building, with some alterations, was the original First Congregational Church that Pa helped build in 1881. On the opposite corner is the original site of the **First School** (13), which Laura and Carrie attended. The building soon became too small for the growing town, and by 1885 it was moved to a location on Third Street (14). Eventually, the school was converted to a home. A block away from the school, at the corner of Loftus Avenue and Fourth Street, is the site of Almanzo and Laura's first house (15). Rose wrote about this house in *On the Way Home* (Harper & Row, 1962).

Farther west on Third Street is **Washington Park** (16), with a large statue of Father De Smet at its edge.

Ma and Pa's bedroom

At the corner of Harvey Dunn Avenue and Second Street is the **Loftus House** (17), with its original hitching post still in front. Across the street is the site of the **Boast Home** (18), where the Ingallses were often guests. The Boasts moved near the Ingallses when they lived in the Surveyors' House, and the families celebrated New Year's, Thanksgiving, and Christmas together annually.

The rolling prairie land around De Smet has many close ties with Little House characters. Drive north 1.4 miles on Highway 25 and on the left is the **Wilder Homestead** (19), where Rose Wilder Lane was born. A historical marker on the roadside indicates where the Wilder claim shanty once stood atop the lone sloping hill. Almanzo and Laura farmed both the homestead land and the nearby tree claim. To see the **Tree Claim** site (20), drive 1.6 miles north of the homestead on Highway 25. On the left are a few remaining trees from Almanzo's unsuccessful timber claim. The "little gray home in the west," which burned down as Laura told in *The First Four Years*, stood in this area, but the site of the house is not marked. West of the site is the **Almanzo Wilder Memorial Airport**, where small planes can land.

The Big Slough

To see **Spirit Lake** (21), described in *These Happy Golden Years*, continue north on 25 for 6 miles and turn left, driving west for 2 miles. Sioux Indian mounds are evident in the Spirit Lake region, and prairie vistas abound.

De Smet is part of South Dakota's Glacial Lake Region. **Silver Lake** is a pothole lake, and it only fills up when there is a lot of precipitation. The area can be seen across the prairie from Highway 14, just east of De Smet. Just south of 14 is the **Big Slough** and the **Ingalls Homestead Site** (23). Pa sold his land in 1892, but the Memorial Society's native rock monument on a rise of ground marks the original site and explains the family history on this land. The cottonwoods that Pa planted at the end of *By the Shores of Silver Lake* stand tall and green, swaying and whispering in the continual prairie winds of summer. No one knows the fate of the claim shanty that once stood on the homestead.

On land adjoining the homestead are the **Laura Ingalls Wilder Pageant grounds** (24), which allow theatergoers to enjoy the Ingalls land as a background during open-air performances. Farther south and east of the site are the "**Twin Lakes**," Lakes Henry and Thompson (25), where Laura and Almanzo took buggy rides. Lake Thompson is now South Dakota's largest natural lake, and a resurgence of fishing and water recreation has developed in recent years.

Homestead marker

The Ingalls Homestead Site

Driving west from De Smet on Highway 14, the **Laura Ingalls Wilder Elementary School** (26) is on the right. On the edge of town is the **Congregational Church** (27). Its modern building replaced the original church; but a link with the past is the original 1883 bell, which hangs in a freestanding tower near the entrance.

At the church, turn left on Prairie Avenue to see the **De Smet Cemetery** (28). Names in the cemetery read like the cast of characters in the Little House books set in De Smet: Boast, Loftus, Fuller, Brown, and Ingalls. The Ingalls lot can be reached through the last (fifth) entrance road on Prairie Avenue. Proceed to the southern edge of the cemetery. Pa's tall marble

tombstone marks his grave, and smaller footstones were placed for Ma, Mary, Carrie, and the infant son of the Wilders. Grace and her husband, Nathan Dow, are buried nearby.

A panoramic view of the prairie, lakes, and town can be seen from the eastern edge of the cemetery. At Wallum's Corner, the road south leads to the Dow farm, where Grace lived, and to the Dunn homestead, where Harvey Dunn was born. Neither site is marked. A historical marker along Highway 14 near Wallum's Corner

Road by Lake Henry

Charles Ingalls's tombstone

gives the biography of Harvey Dunn (1884–1952), the artist and illustrator who was a native of the area. Both he and Laura knew and respected each other's work. The village of Manchester, just off Highway 14, vanished from the landscape during a devastating tornado in June, 2003. Laura helped Mrs. McKee homestead on land near here, as she told in *These Happy Golden Years*.

The Laura Ingalls Wilder Memorial Society is open year-round. Please contact the society for its hours. Admission: $7 for adults; $4 for children 5–12. For information on the tours and information on membership in the society, visit

the society online at www.discover-laura.org/index.html, or contact the Laura Ingalls Wilder Memorial Society, P.O. Box 426, De Smet, SD 57231; tel. 605-854-3383 or 800-880-3383. For more information about De Smet in general, contact the De Smet Chamber of Commerce, P.O. Box 105, De Smet, SD 57231; tel. 866-528-7273, or visit www.desmetsd.com. Always include a stamp with your inquiry.

The highlight of the summer tourist season in De Smet is the **Laura Ingalls Wilder Pageant**, which has been held annually since 1971. A volunteer cast of area performers depicts the life of the Ingalls family and their friends on three weekends in July. The authentic costumes and props, the use of live animals, and the prairie setting make this a favorite among summer visitors. For more information,

Caroline Ingalls's grave

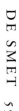

dates, and admission prices, visit www.desmetpageant.org, or write to the Laura Ingalls Wilder Pageant Society, P.O. Box 154, De Smet, SD 57231; tel. 800-776-3594.

WHAT TO DO AROUND DE SMET

Many visitors who see De Smet may wish to take in the many other wonderful pioneer experiences South Dakota has to offer. The state, by the way, is officially divided into "East River" and "West River" by the Missouri River. Time changes at the river from Central Standard to Mountain Standard, an important point for tourists to note, especially if they are racing to visit an attraction before closing time.

Along Highway 14, at the junction of 1-29, is **Brookings**, 37 miles east of De Smet. It is the home of South Dakota State University and has a number of worthwhile attractions, as well as many lodging and eating opportunities for travelers. The **South Dakota Art Museum** (www3.sdstate.edu/administration/southdakotaartmuseum/) on the university campus is open Mon.–Fri., 10 to 5; Sat., 10 to 4; Sun., 12 to 4. Admission is free. Of particular interest is the Harvey Dunn Collection. Painted in the first half of the century, this collection depicts homesteading life near De Smet. Also on the campus is the **State Agricultural Heritage Museum**, open Mon.–Sat., 10 to 5; Sun., 1 to 5. Admission is free. Exhibits depict the agricultural and rural lifestyle that is so much a part of South Dakota. Within the museum is also an 1880s claim shanty from the De Smet area, outfitted with typical furnishings. Brookings's best-attended annual event is the **Summer Arts Festival**, held annually in early July. The festival is held on the second weekend in July and features a juried selection of artisan crafts, including quilts, jewelry, and pottery. There is always a children's program and featured entertainment, which in past years has included Renaissance jousts, singing groups, and plays performed by college theater troupes. For information about the festival, visit www.bsaf.com. For more information about Brookings, contact the Chamber of Commerce, P.O. Box 431, Brookings, SD 57006; tel. 605-692-6125, or visit www.brookingssd.com.

Madison, at the junction of Highways 81 and 34, is the home of **Prairie Village**, a collection of forty historic prairie buildings, each brimming with authentic antique furniture and decor. There is an hour-long self-guided walking tour around the village. On the grounds there are an old-fashioned carousel, picnic tables, a gazebo for eating, and a gift shop. At the end of August every year there is a **"Steam Threshing Jamboree"** weekend, which features old-fashioned steam threshers and other handicraft exhibits. For information about the village, contact the Chamber of Commerce, 315 S. Egan Ave., Madison, SD 57042; tel. 605-256-2454; fax 605-256-9606; or visit www.prairievillage.org or www.madison.sd.us.

South Dakota's state capital, **Pierre** (pronounced "Peer"), is located 150 miles west of De Smet, via Highway 14. During the early days of auto tourism, Highway 14 was promoted as the best route to Yellowstone. Laura and Almanzo Wilder drove this route from East River to West River, South Dakota, in 1931, 1938, and 1939. They stopped in Pierre, and in 1944, Laura sent Pa's fiddle and other keepsakes to the South Dakota State Historical Society to be exhibited in their museum. (The fiddle was subsequently transferred to Mansfield in 1962.) The society's headquarters is now in the **South Dakota Cultural Heritage Center** in Pierre. The structure is entirely underground to simulate a giant sod house, and it blends in seamlessly with the waves of hills in the surrounding area. The museum is located at 900 Governors Drive (tel. 605-773-3458) and features exhibits on Native American history and the development of the state. Admission: $4 for adults, $3.50 for AAA members, $3 for seniors (over 60); free for children 17 and under.

One hundred and ten miles southwest of Pierre is the **Badlands**

National Park, which is also a national monument. The mission of the park is to protect and preserve the 244,000 acres of bluffs and rolling prairie wilderness—no cars are allowed in much of the park. The park also boasts the world's largest deposit of Oligocene fossils from 27 to 33 million years ago. The park has two campgrounds and many hiking trails. For more information, contact Badlands National Park, 25216 Ben Reifel Rd., P.O. Box 6, Interior, SD 57750; tel. 605-433-5361, or visit www.nps.gov/badl.

At the eastern edge of the Badlands National Park in western South Dakota is the **Prairie Homestead Historic Site**, an attraction bound to captivate Little House fans. The half-sod, half-frame homestead house, the only authentic one of its kind in the state, graphically depicts the life experienced by pioneers such as the Ingalls family. A sod roof, earth-packed floor, and period furnishings complete the picture of the austere homestead life on the lonely plains. Outbuildings, a

Courtesy of William Anderson

Laura in the Badlands, 1939

Prairie Homestead

pump, antique implements, and a prairie dog village all add to the stark ambience, which is intensified by the endless blowing winds. The site and a visitors' center is open in season. It is located just off Exit 131 on 1-90. For information, visit www.prairiehomestead.com, or write Prairie Homestead Historic Site, 21141 Highway 240, Philip, SD 57567; tel. 605-433-5400. Open sunup until sunset. Admission: $6 for adults; $5 for seniors; $4 for children 11–17; free for children under 11. Family discounts available.

On the other end of the Badlands National Park loop is the town of Wall. Wall is dominated by the world-famous **Wall Drug Store**, which has been dispensing free ice water to travelers since the dusty drought years of the 1930s. Today it is a mecca that caters to nearly every tourist need, an oasis in the sun-burned Badlands. The Wall Drug Store is located at 510 Main Street; tel. 605-279-2175, open 6:30 A.M.– 10 P.M. In the middle of the giant complex of restaurants, souvenir and Western-wear stores, and rock shops is one of the finest sources for Western lore and literature in the region. It is the **Hole in the Wall Bookstore**, located in the drugstore. Carefully selected, hard-to-find books are the norm. Founder Ted Hustead, an admirer of the Little House books, set up a Wilder niche in the bookstore years ago, complete

with wood-carved figures of the Ingalls family.

Beyond Wall, I-90 stretches west into the **Black Hills**, South Dakota's region of pine forests, mountain lakes, and legendary Western history. Laura and Almanzo were among the first wave of automobile tourists in the area, but much earlier, members of Laura's family helped settle the Black Hills. As told in *These Happy Golden Years*, Laura's uncle Thomas Quiner (Ma's brother) was part of the famed Gordon party, which entered the Black Hills seeking gold in 1874. A replica of

The Ingalls Keystone marker

the **Gordon Stockade** stands on the original site settled by the Gordon party, near the town of Custer.

Keystone, located in the Black Hills, is full of Ingalls associations. Originally a mining community located in one of the richest mineral-producing regions of the world, the lure of gold drew Laura's Aunt Polly (Pa's sister) and Uncle Henry Quiner (Ma's brother), and their family to the area in the 1880s. They settled in the now extinct town of Harney, and members of the family are buried nearby. In 1912, Carrie Ingalls, who had been running the local news-paper, married David Swanzey, a Keystone mine owner and prospec-tor. The Swanzey home stood along Keystone's busy tourist street until it was destroyed by fire in 1976, but a marker explaining the Ingalls connec-tion stands next to the post office. David Swanzey and his son are buried in the local cemetery.

Another Keystone attraction is the **1880 Train**. This replica of an early train chugs between Keystone and Hill City during the tourist season for

Mount Rushmore

a two-hour journey through majestic Black Hills scenery. For more information, visit www.1880train.com; tel. 605-574-2222.

Perhaps Keystone's most famous site is **Mount Rushmore National Memorial**, only 2 miles away from Keystone. On visits during the 1930s, Laura and Almanzo watched the sculptures of Washington, Jefferson, Lincoln, and Theodore Roosevelt being carved on the mountainside. Mount Rushmore owes its name to Carrie's husband, David Swanzey. When he accompanied a New York lawyer, Charles Rushmore, on a ride through the hills, Mr. Swanzey named the granite peak after his guest. The name stuck.

The original town of Keystone was located around a bend from where most of the tourist activity is centered

today. Called **Old Keystone**, this site of the original town has several Little House associations. The historic **Halley Store**, dating to 1880 and frequented by Carrie and her husband, is still in operation. Services are still held at the 1895 **Congregational Church**, located on Blair and Second Streets; Carrie was active in this church until her death in 1946.

Near the church is the **Keystone Historical Museum and School**. The attractive Victorian school was completed in 1899, and was a focal point for community activities. The building now houses the Keystone Area Historical Society and a museum. This museum has exhibits on the town's early history, mining, the carving of Mount Rushmore, and the Badlands rocks and minerals. For Little House fans, there are displays containing

The Keystone Historical Museum and School

memorabilia of Carrie Ingalls Swanzey and belongings of the Ingalls family. The museum is open June–Aug., Mon.–Sat., 10 to 3. Admission is by donation. For information about the society, visit www.keystonechamber.com/kahs/museum.html, or write to 410 Third Street, Keystone, SD 57751; tel. 605-666-4494. For more information on any of the Keystone attractions, visit www.keystonechamber.com, or call 800-456-3345.

The South Dakota Vacation Guide, which gives resource information on the entire state, is updated each year by the South Dakota Department of Tourism, Capitol Lake Plaza, 711 E. Wells Ave., c/o 500 E. Capitol Ave., Pierre, SD 57501; tel. 800-S-DAKOTA, or visit www.travelsd.com.

WHERE TO EAT AND STAY

De Smet has a variety of cafes and fast-food spots. The **Oxbow Restaurant**, open daily 6 A.M.–8:30 P.M., serves breakfast, lunch, and dinner at very low prices (Highway 14 and Calumet Ave.; tel. 605-854-9988). Downtown De Smet and most of the Little House sites are within walking distance. **Country View** (www.countryview.biz; 611 Seventh

Street SW.; tel. 605-854-3134) is in the local country club and is open to the public for lunch and dinner.

There are also several places to stay in the immediate De Smet area. **The Super 8 De Smet** is located at 288 Hwy 14 East. **The Cottage Inn Motel** is located across the street from the Oxbow Restaurant near downtown De Smet (www.cottageinnmotel.com; tel. 800-848-0215). **The Prairie House Manor Bed and Breakfast**, on Poinsett and Third, has accommodations for fifteen in the historic main house (www.prairiehousemanor.com; RR 2, Box 61A, De Smet, SD 57231; tel. 800-297-2416 or 605-854-9131). **The Heritage House Bed and Breakfast** is on the corner of Second Street and Calumet Avenue. Visit www.bbonline.com/sd/heritage for more information.

Camping in De Smet is available at the **SPOT campgrounds**, with over fifty hookups (305 Highway 14E, De Smet, SD 57231; tel. 605-854-3982; call in the evening). Camping is also available at the Ingalls Homestead (www.ingallshomestead.com; tel.

800-776-3594).

Keystone has a variety of motels, lodges, and campsites available. For listings, visit www.keystonechamber.com, or write Keystone Chamber of Commerce, P.O. Box 653, Keystone, SD 57751; tel. 605-666-4896. Rapid City, 23 miles distant, has lodging for four thousand. Visit www.rcgov.com for more information. Because this area is a tourist mecca, lodging is sometimes booked solid in peak times. Advance reservations are recommended!

How to Get There

De Smet is located at the junction of Highway 14 and Highway 25. A stretch of Highway 14 near De Smet has been designated as the Laura Ingalls Wilder Memorial Highway. Interstate signs on I-29 direct travelers to De Smet, which is 33 miles east of Huron, 37 miles west of Brookings, and 90 miles from Sioux Falls. The closest Little House site to De Smet is Walnut Grove, Minnesota, about 110 miles away.

MANSFIELD, MISSOURI, AND THE ROCKY RIDGE YEARS

LAURA, ALMANZO, AND ROCKY RIDGE FARM

After struggling for several years in De Smet, South Dakota, and after a brief and unhappy move to Westville, Florida, Laura and Almanzo decided to move to a place kinder to farmers than De Smet. Lured by promotional literature advertising the Ozarks as a good region for small-scale farming, the Wilders set off once again in a covered wagon in search of a better life. Laura describes this journey in *On the Way Home.*

The Wilders ended what would be their last journey in Mansfield, Missouri. The town, established 1881–1882, was a growing community. A 40-acre plot of land a mile east of the Mansfield town square became the final home of the Wilder family. The purchase price was $400;

the paperwork, all in Laura's name, was signed on September 21, 1894.

Like most of the Ozarks, the site consisted of ridges, slopes, and chiseled rocks. Laura aptly named the Wilder land Rocky Ridge Farm. The Wilders' first home on the farm, a one-room log cabin, stood at the top of a wooded knoll. Eventually, Laura and Almanzo built a larger farmhouse nearby, and the log cabin has long since vanished.

Over time, Laura and Almanzo added onto both the farmhouse and the farm itself. Rocky Ridge Farm grew to include approximately 200 acres. While it was not a large farm, Rocky Ridge was, nonetheless, known for its up-to-date methods in raising cows, chickens, and fruits. In 1913, after many years of labor, Laura and Almanzo put the final addition on their rambling white frame home. This was their last little house, and it

Left: Laura's Rocky Ridge farmhouse

was here that Laura wrote many of her Little House books.

THE FOUNDING OF THE SITE

Rocky Ridge was famous even before Laura wrote her Little House books. First, it became known because the structure of the house itself was unique. Then during the 1920s and 1930s, the farm became known as the home of Rose Wilder Lane, whose short stories and books were increasingly popular. Finally, when the Little House books were published in the 1930s and 1940s, Rocky Ridge Farm became renowned as the home of Laura Ingalls Wilder. Many readers came to stare and photograph the house from the road; many more rapped on the screen door and were welcomed in for a visit by the author herself.

Even before her death, local friends and admirers from afar expressed the quiet hope that the Wilder home could be preserved as a memorial to Laura Ingalls Wilder. Laura was aware of the sentiment and was pleased, if humbly dubious that it could happen.

Within days of her death in February 1957, Laura's friends combined with community leaders in Mansfield to form the Laura Ingalls Wilder Home Association, dedicated to the preservation of the Rocky Ridge farmhouse. Rose Wilder Lane cooperated completely with the plan to preserve her parents' home. She contributed the entire treasure trove of memorabilia and furnishings in the house to the newly formed association.

Before the work of the association could progress, the house and surrounding grounds needed to be reacquired, as Laura and Almanzo had sold the land and house, retaining only a life-estate deed. Rose and the fifty-six original founding members contributed the money needed to begin the preservation project. The first open house was held in May 1957. Since that date, the steady flow of visitors from the United States and, indeed, from all over the world who have arrived to tour the Wilder home has been uninterrupted.

The farmhouse

Rose was greatly interested in the preservation of the family home, but insisted that her role be a silent one. She claimed no recognition in the memorial to her parents. She offered ready advice to the first curators, Lewis and Irene Lichty, and in 1963 she offered to build a curators' house on the property.

Only after Rose's death in 1968 did her name and accomplishments receive more prominent recognition on Rocky Ridge Farm. Her heir, Roger Lea MacBride, contributed much of Rose's own memorabilia to the expanding memorial. In 1971, a museum building was constructed near the historic Wilder house to exhibit Rose's own memorabilia.

In 1992, the United States Department of the Interior designated the Wilder home as a National Landmark, America's highest honor for historic properties.

WHAT TO SEE AND DO

A mile from Mansfield, via the curving Highway A, is the **Laura Ingalls Wilder Historic Home and Museum**. The white farmhouse sits, half turned, atop a gently sloping ridge. The three focal points for visitors are located on the spacious

Pa's fiddle and other Little House memorabilia

honors, first editions of her books, and the stacks of original manuscripts, all penciled into 5-cent, orange-covered, lined school tablets. Five of the book manuscripts are on display, along with examples of Laura's earlier journal articles.

A separate wing of the museum features the life and career of Rose Wilder Lane. Her various desks, her voluminous needlework, collectibles gathered on world travels, and furnishings from her Danbury, Connecticut, home reflect a life that, though far more cosmopolitan than her parents', nonetheless retains a marked homespun character. Her World War II canning journal is on display; Rose stated that growing her own food gave her more satisfaction than writing a book.

The chief artifact in the museum—indeed, the point of pilgrimage for many—is Pa Ingalls's fiddle. The honey-brown violin is believed to be German made, from the 1850s. Its role in the Ingalls family history and the Little House books cannot be overstated. Visitors' reverent reactions attest to the joy, inspiration,

wooded grounds: the Little House Museum, the bookstore, and the original house.

Tours begin at the museum, which is filled with relics that span over a century of the Ingalls and Wilder family life, from the marriage of Charles Ingalls and Caroline Quiner in 1860 to the round-the-globe trip planned by their granddaughter Rose just before her death. The focus, however, is on Laura and Almanzo, and the lives they led on Rocky Ridge. Exhibits include clothing, keepsakes, tools, Laura's needlework, items mentioned in the Little House books, and possessions that belonged to characters in the stories. One display concentrates on Laura's writing, her courage, and faith that poured from the fiddle and are still communicated in the pages of Laura Ingalls Wilder's books.

Next door to the museum is the **Little House Bookstore**. You can buy all of Laura's Little House books there, as well as the many other Little House publications and souvenirs.

ROOM BY ROOM AT ROCKY RIDGE

One can easily spend an hour or two in the museum and bookstore, but the crowning experience at Rocky Ridge Farm is to step into the historic house itself. It has been

Laura's kitchen

preserved exactly as the Wilders kept it in the 1940s and 1950s. None of the household items have been removed, and nothing has been added to the place the Wilders called home for most of their lives.

From the museum it is only a few steps onto the narrow side porch and so into the house. Laura and Almanzo began building the house in 1896; they completed it in 1913. Laura worked along with her husband felling huge oak trees to use for lumber; they gathered stones from their land to build the foundation and chimney. Laura believed that a country home should grow out of the natural materials on the land where it stood.

The sprawling house consists of ten rooms. Its shape is irregular. Floors and walls slope and slant and there are few straight lines. Since the house was built as a series of additions, there are no hallways; rooms open onto one another. In effect, Rocky Ridge farmhouse has as much variation in color and texture as a patchwork quilt.

The **kitchen** is the starting point for a house tour. It is a compact room,

Some of Laura's kitchen utensils

full of color—yellow enamel, pink Depression glass, a green wood range, gaudy pot holders and towels. When the kitchen was finished around 1920, it was considered modern. Some years earlier, Almanzo had diverted an upland spring into the circa 1905 stove, thus giving Laura hot running water. Built-in cupboards and low countertops line the walls. They were tailored by Almanzo to fit his wife's five-foot stature. Later, Laura and Almanzo added more modern appliances, including a 1930s two-burner electric stove.

Many well-worn kitchen utensils are in plain sight on counters and in cupboards. Over the years, Laura and Almanzo amassed many pieces of dishware. On exhibit are examples of Laura's Blue Willoware, Haviland china, and a set of 1932 everyday dishes.

Laura called the farm kitchen her workshop. There she canned garden produce, skimmed cream, kneaded bread, sorted eggs, and cooked for family, friends, and farm workers. As Laura worked in the kitchen, she was able to look out on the rolling hills and trees outside, which are still visible from the windows. Laura was known as an excellent cook and entertainer.

The tidy and well-appointed kitchen attests to Laura's skill as a cook and a farm wife, but it was also where she spread out her orange tablets to write. She wrote whenever she could grab time "between washing dishes and

The family clock

getting dinner . . . anytime I could."

On the way from the kitchen to the **dining room**, visitors can see a leftover from the earliest construction of the house. It is a narrow, ladderlike staircase used by Rose to reach her sleeping loft above.

The dining room combines the homemade with the store-bought. Originally the dining room served as Laura and Almanzo's kitchen, and one whole wall consists of drawers and cupboards made by Almanzo for storing food and dishes. Later, when the present kitchen was built, the same cabinets became an extended sideboard for the dining room.

The large dining table (circa 1928) is flanked by Laura's favorite rocking chair. This table became a clearinghouse for Laura's daily load of fan mail, which she diligently read and answered.

During the winter, the oil-burning heater in the corner of the room warmed the dining room, bedroom, and kitchen; the rest of the house was shut off during the winter to conserve heat. Behind the heater, on a corner shelf, is the clock, brought to Mansfield from De Smet in 1894. This clock is described in *The First Four Years.* Almanzo wound the clock nightly; it still ticks and chimes the hours.

The dining room doubled as a sitting room, so several chairs line the walls. One is a straight-back Windsor, another a homemade replica of the

The dining room

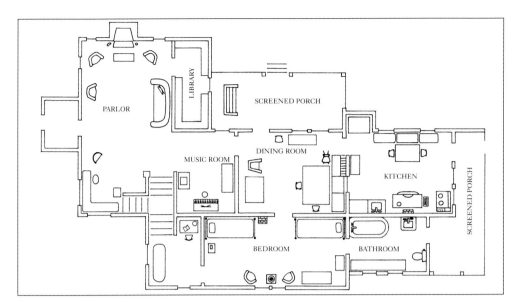

The Rocky Ridge farmhouse floor plan

slant-back Adirondack style. Here callers often visited informally with the Wilders.

One door from the dining room opens onto the screened porch, with a suspended swing. The other leads to the Wilders' **bedroom**.

The long, narrow bedroom has metal twin beds, another homemade chair, vanity tables, and the original patterned linoleum rug on the floor. Currier and Ives prints and assorted Western scenes adorn the walls. Through a door, the **bathroom** can be seen. Indoor plumbing was added to the house around 1920, and the bath-

room was last modernized in 1956.

Following her husband's death, Laura began sleeping in Almanzo's bed; this was one of her expressions of loneliness. She also never emptied Almanzo's medicine box, which still contains bottles of Vicks, eyedrops, cod-liver oil, Listerine, and a hand-labeled elixir marked "Black Draught." The box rests on a table Almanzo built, which has a forked branch as its base. Almanzo's cane collection, which stands in the corner, displays his ability to turn native wood into craftsmanship.

During her years of authorship,

Laura would creep, deep in the night, into her **writing study**, which adjoins the bedroom. She sometimes awoke with ideas and paragraphs already formed and was determined to capture them on paper, despite the late hour. At her dainty drop-leaf desk, she drafted many of the chapters in her life story. The nearby "fainting couch" (circa 1900) provided a place to rest during writing stints. It is called a fainting couch because in the nineteenth century, tightly corseted women often felt faint from lack of oxygen and needed to lie down on couches to recover their breath.

Laura's desk is still filled with her notepads stuck in cubbyholes and with

Laura's desk

the pencil stubs she used. She was frugal with both pencil and paper.

From the writing study, a few steps take you to a landing, which has an oak staircase leading to the **upstairs**, where there is a guest room, a long all-purpose room, and a sleeping porch. The sleeping porch, with eleven windows and a door leading to a tiny balcony, became Rose Wilder Lane's bedroom and office during some of her most prolific periods of writing. The original furnishings are still there, including her desk and a pencil sharpener attached to the windowsill. At present, however, these upstairs rooms are not open to tours.

From the stairway landing, visitors catch their first glimpse of the **parlor**. Completed in 1913, the large oblong room features stout beams across the ceiling, oak paneling, and picture windows that provide beautiful views of the surrounding countryside. The parlor was carefully planned by Laura; and the boxy pillars, liberal use of paneling, and beams suggest that some outside input inspired her design of the room. Possibly Laura was

The parlor

influenced by the popular Mission style of the period and the work of Frank Lloyd Wright. Laura once recalled that her finished parlor looked so rustic and woodsy that a visiting neighbor sniffed, "Hm! Must've thought she was building a mill!"

The fireplace is formed from three huge stones found on the farm. Almanzo initially refused to move them and bought a load of brick to build the fireplace instead. Laura said, "For the only time in my life I made use of a woman's time-honored weapon, tears." The fireplace was ultimately built exactly to her specifications. A polished oak mantelpiece tops it; hand-forged andirons add to the rustic creation. Outside, the chimney is a work of rural art, a mixture of stone-embedded fossils and white, brown, and tan rock intermixed.

Another of Laura's ambitions for her home was that there be plenty of space for books. A corner of the parlor was walled off with five-foot-high shelves. Over three hundred of the Wilders'

The stone fireplace

books are still intact in the library nook. Laura also displayed her many literary awards on these shelves, along with her daughter's graduation portrait.

Opposite the library is a larger nook called the **music room**. The 1890 pump organ, probably bought so that Rose could take music lessons, has been widely mistaken for Mary's organ from the Ingalls home in De Smet. The Wilder organ is still filled with old songbooks, which were used by Laura for reference as she selected song lyrics to use in her Little House books. Next to the organ is the 1928 Electrola, a record player designed to use wooden needles. The buffet in the room provided storage space for stacks of vintage records. The Wilders had eclectic tastes in music, and their records are a mix of cowboy and Western songs, operas, humorous songs, and popu-

The music room

lar orchestras and vocalists of the era. Above the buffet is a striking oil portrait of Rose from 1917, done by San Francisco artist Lydia Gibson.

The other notable work of art in the parlor is the oil painting that depicts a young couple in a covered wagon. The artist was W.H.D. Koerner (1878–1938), who created the illustration for Rose's *Let the Hurricane Roar* when it appeared as a serial in *The Saturday Evening Post* in 1932. The original canvas was presented to the author later that year.

The many tourists who have walked on the brown wool carpet of the parlor since Laura's home was opened to the public were preceded by a procession of visitors during the Wilders' times. The house was a center

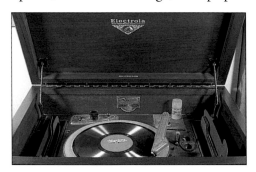

Laura's Electrola

Almanzo's cypress table

of hospitality, with square dances, costume parties, club meetings, card parties, and drop-in company. There was plenty of seating for guests provided by the collection of rocking chairs, comfortably lumpy upholstered chairs and couch, a fireplace bench, and a window seat. Most of the furniture dates to 1928, although there are a few antiques from earlier eras in the family. One of the finest pieces of Almanzo's craft work is in the parlor. It is the highly polished table he created from a cypress stump while he and Laura lived in Westville, Florida. A few hooked rugs and a horse design on a pillow are also his work; during winter months he did hookwork to keep occupied. The many doilies, pillows, and arm covers in the parlor were made by Laura.

"It fits you like it is your shell," remarked a friend to Laura of her parlor. The Wilder hospitality seems to live on in the warm atmosphere of this room.

THE GROUNDS

The wooded grounds that make up Rocky Ridge Farm are available for unlimited access during open hours. Visitors exit from the parlor door onto one of the four porches surrounding the house. Benches in restful settings under the oaks provide places for relaxing and viewing the rolling Ozark landscape. Behind the house is the **ravine**, with its massive rock formations and a stream that trickles through the gulch.

Two other houses on the original Wilder land have been acquired by the Laura Ingalls Wilder Home Association. One is directly opposite the house-museum complex, across Highway A. It is a stone cottage built in 1928 for tenant farmer use. The Wilders were visitors there. It is

The ravine

not available for touring. Across the wooded ridge is the **Rock House**, also built in 1928. This English-style cottage, consisting of six rooms, was built as a gift from Rose to her parents who lived there from 1928 to 1936, while the first four Little House books were written. The Rock House has been restored and is open for tours.

The Laura Ingalls Wilder Historic Home and Museum is open Mar. 1–Nov. 15, Mon.–Sat., 9 to 5; Sun., 12:30 to 5:30; and Nov. 16–mid-Dec. by appointment only. Admission: $8 for adults, $6 for seniors (over 65), $4 for children 6–18; children under 6 free.

For further information, a newsletter, or a bookstore catalog, visit www.lauraingallswilderhome.com, or contact the Laura Ingalls Wilder Historic Home and Museum, 3068 Highway A, Mansfield, MO 65704; tel. 417-924-3626 or 877-924-7126. Always enclose a stamp with your inquiry.

In addition to the Laura Ingalls Wilder Historic Home and Museum, Mansfield is host to several annual events related to Laura and Little House. In late August and early

The Rock House

Courtesy of William Anderson

September, Mansfield's **Ozark Mountain Players** stage a musical pageant based on stories from the Little House books. Write the Ozark Mountain Players, P.O. Box 113, Mansfield, MO 65704 for details, or visit them online at www.mansfield-chamber.com/ozarkmtnplayers.com.

The third weekend of September is traditionally the town of Mansfield's **Laura Ingalls Wilder Festival**. A variety of entertaining events are scheduled during this fall festival. Pa's original fiddle is customarily played on this day. For exact dates and details on the celebration, call or write the Laura Ingalls Wilder Historic Home and Museum.

WHAT TO SEE IN AND AROUND MANSFIELD

Mansfield was Laura's home for sixty-three years. She grew to love the little town in the Ozarks, and its people returned her affection. In 1951, the local library was named for her. After changing locations several times, the **Laura Ingalls Wilder Library** is now north of Commercial Street, the main avenue of the town, on Highway 5. The library exhibits a case containing signed books and other memorabilia.

The current library stands on the approximate site of the 1899 Methodist Church building, now demolished. The Wilders were active in this congregation, but also knew the **Cumberland Presbyterian Church** building well, as the Methodists used to meet in this building before their first church was built. This landmark, built in 1884 south of the town square, is one of the oldest buildings in town. The oldest continuous business in town is **The Bank of Mansfield**, established in 1892. The Wilders passed under its impressive portal often.

The houses along the eastern end of Commercial Street have historic ties with the Wilders. At the corner of Commercial and Ash is the **town house** where the Wilders lived in the early 1900s. It has now been covered with rock siding. In the next block is a circa 1890 two-story frame house with a cupola. It was the cupola that

The Wilders' town house

attracted Rose Wilder's attention as the family drove out to their new farm for the first time. The cupola house was later the longtime home of the Craig family, friends of the Wilders. Rose's Ozark novel *Hill Billy* is based on the life of N. J. Craig, a local lawyer and banker. Neither house is available for touring, but can be readily noted by visitors en route to the Wilder Home and Museum.

On Lincoln Street, near the **Laura Ingalls Wilder Elementary School**, is the **Mansfield Cemetery**. This is the last resting place for Laura and Almanzo Wilder. The family plot is in the center section of the graveyard, surrounded with simple posts and chain. Rose's remains were added to the family plot in 1968. The cemetery tombstones bear names of many other local residents who shared friendships with the Wilder family, including the 1897 grave of Frank Cooley, a close friend who accompanied the Wilders on the 1894 trek from De Smet to Mansfield.

The center of town in Mansfield is its **town square**, bounded on two sides by rows of century-old brick structures. As it was during the Wilder era, the square is a gathering spot for Mansfield's 1,500 residents to meet, celebrate, or simply relax under the shady trees. In 1993, a bronze bust portrait of Laura, a duplicate of which is in the state capitol in Jefferson

City, was placed in the square as a memorial. There the statue surveys the traffic headed to her home with a slightly bemused expression that seems to reflect Laura's own real-life incredulity about the widespread fame achieved late in her life.

Just 50 miles west of Mansfield on Highway 60 is **Springfield**, Missouri, advertised as "The Gateway City to Ozark Mountain Country." Springfield offers a numerous array of restaurants, entertainment, and lodgings. For further information on its attractions, write Springfield Missouri Convention and Visitors Bureau, 3315 E. Battlefield Road, Springfield, MO 65804; tel. 800-678-8767 or 417-881-5300, or visit www.springfieldmo.org.

Thirty-five miles south of Springfield is **Branson**, dubbed "America's Live Entertainment

The Wilders' grave

Capital." Branson, recently ranked among the top ten favorite family destinations, has dozens of live entertainment theaters featuring a variety of performers. The area surrounding Branson has lakes, theme parks, beautiful Ozark mountain scenery, family-oriented outdoor activities, and shopping. For information, write: Branson/Lakes Area Chamber of Commerce, P.O. Box 1897, Branson, MO 65615; tel. 800-214-3661, or visit www.branson-chamber.com.

WHERE TO EAT AND STAY

The **Little House Buffet** (at the intersection of W. Business Route 60 and Highway 5; tel. 417-924-3334) has recently been enlarged to accommodate up to 150 diners. It is open seven days a week, 6 A.M.–2 P.M. Other cafes are located around Mansfield's town square and offer a variety of small-town eating experiences.

Mansfield has only one motel, **Little House Inn**, a step away from

Mansfield's statue of Laura

the Little House Buffet (just off the Mansfield exit on Highway 60; tel. 417-924-3531).

Along Highway 60 heading east about thirty minutes from Mansfield is the town of **Mountain Grove**. Several chain motels and fast-food restaurants are there, including a Best Western, Days Inn, and McDonald's.

For a unique vacation experience in the Ozarks, travelers may want to visit the **Rainbow Trout and Game Ranch** (P.O. Box 100, Rockbridge, MO 65741; tel. 417-679-3619). Deep in wooded hills, near historic Rockbridge Mill, this rustic resort has motel units, trout fishing, and a restaurant specializing in freshwater fish. To reach the resort, follow Highway 5 south from Mansfield for about 27 miles and turn left (east) on Highway N for another 15 miles.

HOW TO GET THERE

Mansfield is located off Highway 60, just over four hours by car from Kansas City or St. Louis. The nearest major city is Springfield, 50 miles to the west, which is served by Springfield-Branson Regional Airport, with fifty daily arrivals. Most major car rental companies offer ground transportation from the airport. The closest Little House site is Independence, Kansas, approximately a half day's drive away.

MALONE, NEW YORK, AND *FARMER BOY*

LAURA, ALMANZO, AND MALONE

In *Farmer Boy*, Laura wrote about Almanzo Wilder's childhood on his family's farm in northern New York State. In the book, Laura described in great detail Almanzo's chores, adventures, and delicious meals. A constant theme running throughout this Little House book, the only one that does not include Laura, is Almanzo's willing and eager participation in working on his family's farm.

The prosperous Wilder farm was located 5 miles from the town of Malone. Almanzo's father, James Wilder, had purchased the 88-acre farm for $340 in 1840. Over the years, Mr. Wilder and his sons built a comfortable farmhouse and substantial barns and outbuildings. It remained the family home until 1875, when the Wilders sold it for $5,000 and moved to Spring Valley, Minnesota (see pages 91–93).

Almanzo never returned to his boyhood home near Malone after his family settled in Spring Valley. However, he had an excellent memory and was able to provide Laura with a fully detailed layout of the farmhouse and of the farm itself, which she then included in *Farmer Boy*. In 1932, Laura and Almanzo's daughter, Rose, visited the old farm and found everything almost exactly as Almanzo had remembered it.

THE FOUNDING OF THE SITE

The credit for bringing the Wilder farm to the attention of Little House fans belongs to Frances Smith and her daughter, Dorothy. In 1949, they discovered that they were distant cousins of Almanzo's, and

Left: The Wilder farmhouse

they wrote to Laura to tell her. After Laura confirmed the relationship, the Smiths began to search the New York countryside, hoping to find the original Wilder farm. A chance meeting with an old schoolmate of Almanzo's led them to the farm, much of which looked as it had in Almanzo's day.

In 1963, when the Franklin County Historical and Museum Society's House of History was established as a museum to preserve the background of Malone and Franklin County, an exhibit was set up in honor of *Farmer Boy*, showing how famous the site and the book had become. In 1966, a historical marker was placed in front of the Wilder farmhouse, which was still occupied. Finally, in 1986, local residents formed the Almanzo and Laura Ingalls Wilder Association, whose pur-

The Wilder farm historical marker

pose was to acquire the Wilder farm. In 1987, the association purchased the acreage and farm buildings and began work on restoring the house.

It took many years of painstaking research and labor to restore the 140-year-old Greek Revival farmhouse. Returning the Wilder home to its original appearance included replacing and reconstructing several doors and windows, reconstructing the front entrance, and stabilizing the cellar. After the exterior clapboards had been repaired and replaced, the house was painted red, as it had been during the Wilder years. Interior restoration was done by following descriptions in *Farmer Boy* and by re-creating the typical decor of the time period. For example, a wool loom was used to weave the multicolored carpet in the dining room.

As part of the restoration effort, archeological digs were also carried out. These digs yielded items such as an 1865 two-cent piece and a button dating from 1855. Organic stains in the soil that showed the outlines of the Wilders' original front porch were also discovered.

The kitchen

Over the years, the network of barns and outbuildings behind the Wilder house succumbed to age. The last original structure burned down in 1969 after it was struck by lightning. The Wilder Association has completed the reconstruction of the three barns described in *Farmer Boy*: the Horse Barn, the Big Barn, and the South Barn. An ongoing goal of the Wilder Association is to reconstruct the other outbuildings that once existed on the homestead, including an outhouse, ice-house, etc. A replica of the school-house attended by the Wilder children is another long range goal. All of these projects are dependent upon donations and grants.

WHAT TO SEE AND DO

The **Wilder Homestead** is 5 miles east of downtown Malone, on Stacy Road. Signs mark the way. At the homestead, you can take a guided tour of the house, which has been completely restored and furnished with authentic period pieces.

The pantry

The parlor

Downstairs is the kitchen and an adjoining pantry for storing food. From the kitchen you move into the dining room, the parlor, and two small bedrooms. Mother and Father slept in one of them. Upstairs are two bedrooms, one belonging to Almanzo and Royal and the other to Laura Ann, Alice, and Eliza Jane, which has an antique weaving loom in the center. Located in the attic off of Almanzo's room is a large work space that was Father's workshop.

Picnicking in the Silas Vincent Pavilion is welcome, and there is also a walking trail to the nearby Trout River, in which Almanzo helped wash sheep. In addition, the property also houses a visitors' center, with exhibits of pioneer farm life, and a gift shop.

Each year, the Wilder Association hosts many special events, including crafts demonstrations, entertainment, historical reenactments, and special visits by working Morgan horses. As Laura wrote in *Farmer Boy*, the Wilders preferred the Morgan horses above all other horses. The Morgans were first bred in the neighboring state of Vermont in 1789. These fine-steppers were favorites around Malone and Franklin Counties.

For days and times of operation, admission prices, or information about the Wilder homestead or membership in the Wilder Association, contact the Wilder Association, P.O. Box 283, Malone, NY 12953; tel. 518-483-1207 or 866-438-FARM (3276); send e-mail to almanzo@northnet.org or

The dining room

Upstairs bedroom

visit www.almanzowilderfarm.com.

Malone itself offers a window on nineteenth-century New York life. At the Franklin County Historical and Museum Society's **House of History**, visitors can step into the past. This 1863 Tuscan-style brick building includes Victorian period rooms, craft rooms, and the personal belongings of William A. Wheeler, a Malone native who was vice president under President Rutherford B. Hayes. The museum also has research facilities and is on 51 Milwaukee Street, Malone, NY 12953; tel. 518-483-2750. Open June–Aug. 31, Fri. 1 to 5 and Sat. 1 to 4. Open Sept.–May, Sat. only, 1 to 4.

The **Franklin County Fair**, the largest fair in the north country, still thrives, as it did during Almanzo's day. In *Farmer Boy*, Laura describes the many excitements of Almanzo's trip to the fair, including a first prize for the biggest pumpkin. The fair today is not unlike the fair Almanzo went to; there are still farm animal exhibits, and prizes are still given for produce and baked goods. There are also amusement rides and all kinds of different food to eat. The fairgrounds are located in Malone, and the fair is held for nine days in August. For more information, visit www.frcofair.com, or contact the

Trout River

Malone Chamber of Commerce, 170 E. Main Street, Malone, NY 12953; tel. 518-483-0720.

Malone is located in the northwest foothills of the Adirondack Mountain Range and is about 50 miles north of the summer and winter resort town of Lake Placid, home of the 1980 Winter Olympics. Lakes, wilderness areas, camping, boating, hiking, and, in winter, skiing abound in the area between Malone and Lake Placid. For information about the Lake Placid region and the Adirondack State Park, call 800-447-5224, or visit www.lake-placid.com. For general New York State tourist information, visit http://iloveny.state.ny.us, or call 800-225-5697.

Montreal is only about an hour north of Malone. In fact, Franklin County borders Canada on the north, and the St. Lawrence River can be seen from the Wilder homestead. For information about Montreal, call 800-363-7777.

Burlington, Vermont, is about an hour and a half away from Malone. The drive to this scenic college town, home to the University of Vermont, includes breathtaking views of the Adirondack State Park. There is also a ferry that leaves from Port Kent, New York (about an hour from Malone), travels across Lake Champlain, and docks at Burlington. For ferry information and schedules, call 802-864-9804. For more information about Burlington, visit www.ci.burlington.vt.us.

WHERE TO EAT AND STAY

Malone has a wide variety of restaurants and dining establishments. Among them are **The Village Diner** (tel. 518-483-1719) and **Trombley's Bistro** (tel. 518-483-5512). For the perfect place for families with children, try **Jon's Family Restaurant** (tel. 518-483-6230). All these restaurants are located in or near the downtown Malone area.

Motels include **Clark's Motel** (E. Main Street Road; tel. 518-483-0900); **Dreamland Motel** (E. Main Street; tel. 518-483-1806; **Sunset Motel** (3899 State Rte. 11; tel. 518-

Front view of the house

483-3367); **Econo Lodge** (W. Main Street; tel. 518-483-0500); **Four Seasons Motel** (W. Main Street; tel. 518-483-3490); **Gateway Motel** (Route 30 S., Finney Boulevard; tel. 518-483-4200); and **Malone Super 8** (42 Finney Boulevard; tel. 518-483-8123). The city address for all is Malone, NY 12953.

The **Kilburn Manor** (59 Milwaukee Street, Malone, NY 12953; www.kilburnmanor.com; tel. 518-483-4891) is a Greek Revival house dating back to the 1820s that has been transformed into a bed-and-breakfast. It was once the home of Congressman Clarence Kilburn, a twentieth-century Malone resident who promoted *Farmer Boy* and corresponded with Laura Ingalls Wilder.

HOW TO GET THERE

Malone is located between Interstates 81 and 87. Montreal is about 70 miles to the north; New York City and Boston are both more than 300 miles distant. From the north or south, get onto Route 11 West, which goes right through Malone.

Airports located in Montreal or Burlington, Vermont, provide the closest major air service. Rental cars are readily available at each airport. Adirondack Trailways provides bus service to the area. For information on bus fares and schedules, call 800-858-8555.

> *"Mr. Wilder liked the country so well that he*
> *bought a farm near Spring Valley."*
> —LAURA INGALLS WILDER

SPRING VALLEY, MINNESOTA, AND THE WILDER FAMILY

LAURA, ALMANZO, AND SPRING VALLEY

The southeastern Minnesota community of Spring Valley was only mentioned once in the Little House books (in *Little Town on the Prairie*), but for Laura and Almanzo it had many associations. In the early 1870s, James Wilder purchased farmland on the north edge of Spring Valley. When the family property in Malone was sold, Royal and Almanzo, who had stayed behind to tend the farm, rejoined the rest of the family in Spring Valley. They quickly established a farm just as successful as the one they had left behind.

Even after Almanzo moved west to Dakota Territory with Royal and Eliza Jane, Spring Valley remained a place to visit between stints of "holding down" their homestead claims near De Smet.

After the hard months Laura recorded in *The First Four Years*, Almanzo, Laura, and Rose moved for a time to Spring Valley, living with Almanzo's parents on the farm. By then the place had an oversized, comfortable house surrounded by oak trees. Nearly vanquished by illness and crop failures in South Dakota, Almanzo and Laura welcomed the year of rest with Almanzo's parents. They lived there from May 1890 through October 1891, before moving briefly to Florida and then back to De Smet.

Almanzo's parents lived on in Spring Valley until 1898, celebrating their golden wedding anniversary and Eliza Jane's wedding at their farmhouse.

Near the end of their lives, the Wilders left Spring Valley to live near relatives in Louisiana. The graves of James (1813–1899) and Angeline

Left: The Wilders' Spring Valley farmhouse

(1819–1905) are in the Old Crowley Cemetery in Crowley, Louisiana.

Royal remained as Spring Valley's only Wilder. He was a merchant, operating variety stores in several locations. He died in 1925 and is buried in the local cemetery.

The Spring Valley Community Historical Society works to preserve both the history of the area and the connection with the Wilders. Over the years, a trickle of Little House fans has grown to a steady stream of tourists who leave no site unvisited that once was home to the Wilders.

WHAT TO SEE AND DO

The first hope of Wilder fans is to visit the family farm. Unfortunately, this cannot be done. The comfortable house was razed in 1926, although a wooden barn, set on a high rock wall, is believed to be the one used by the Wilders. The farm, located on Tracy Road near the outskirts of Spring Valley, is privately owned. No tours or visitors are allowed.

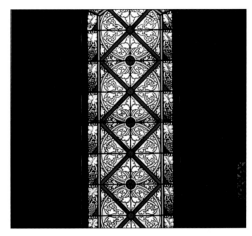

Methodist Church window

Fortunately, the Spring Valley Community Historical Society is aware of the interest in the Wilders, and the **Methodist Church Museum**, located at 221 West Courtland Street, offers Wilder and pioneer information. The Victorian Gothic church has Wilder connections; members of the family attended here, and when the building was started in 1876, they were contributors. The church, on the National Register of Historic Places, is remarkable for its series of twenty-three stained glass windows dating to 1715. Exhibits in the church tell the story of the town's pioneers, businesses, and general history. A marker in the yard explains the Wilder associations.

Connected to the church museum is the **Washburn-Zittelman House Museum,** also maintained by the Historical Society. The house museum offers a glimpse of the farming life the Wilders knew in Spring Valley. Artifacts and furnishings are displayed in ten areas; period rooms, as well as quilts, antique clothing, toys, and dolls are on exhibit. The church and museum are located next door to each other at 221 and 220 West Courtland, Spring Valley, MN 55975; tel. 507-346-7659. Open daily from Memorial Day weekend to Labor Day, 10 to 4. Open weekends Sept.–Oct., 10 to 4. Tours are offered by appointment. Admission: adults, $3 for church only, $5 for church and house; children, $1 for church only, $2 for church and house.

For more information, write to the Spring Valley Community Historical Society Inc., 221 West Courtland Street, Spring Valley, MN 55975; tel. 507-346-7659; or Spring Valley Chamber of Commerce, P.O. Box 13, Spring Valley, MN 55975; tel. 507-346-1015.

WHERE TO EAT AND STAY

Spring Valley has several restaurants, including **Elaine's** (Main St. and Broadway; tel. 507-346-7492), which serves breakfast, lunch, and dinner and is open every day; and **Big Bob's** (136 N. Broadway; tel. 507-346-9848), which offers specials such as lasagna and ribs. Lodging in Spring Valley is available at **Shady Rest Motel** (Highways 16 and 63 N.; tel. 507-346-2625); **Motel 66** (612 N. Huron Ave.; tel. 507-346-9993); **Park View Motel** (1401 S. Section Ave.; tel. 507-346-2861.)

HOW TO GET THERE

Spring Valley is at the junction of Highways 16 and 63. It is 26 miles south of Rochester and 110 miles south of the Twin Cities. It is close to several other Little House sites. Burr Oak, Iowa, is a forty-five-minute drive from Spring Valley, and Pepin, Wisconsin, is approximately two to three hours away by car.

"I have never cared for cities but San Francisco is simply the most beautiful thing."
—LAURA INGALLS WILDER

OTHER SITES OF LITTLE HOUSE INTEREST

ROSE WILDER LANE LOCALES

San Francisco, California, was Rose's home base periodically during the 1910s. There she launched a successful career in journalism at the *San Francisco Bulletin*. Her life during that era is described in *West From Home* (Harper & Row, 1974). During the 1915 World's Fair Rose was living in an apartment house atop Russian Hill, at 1018 Vallejo Street. The architectural landmark is still standing, and can be viewed from the street.

New York City frequently lured Rose during her long career in publishing. She made extended stays in the city and in 1919 lived in Greenwich Village. The three-story building where she rented an apartment is still at 31 Jones Street. In 1939, she leased what she affectionately called her "slum apartment" at 550 East Sixteenth Street. She spent several winters there, using the place as a New York base. This building has since been razed.

Danbury, Connecticut, became Rose's permanent residence in 1938. She bought and extensively remodeled a simple farmhouse in the rural King Street district, and there she carried on her literary life for the next thirty years. Rose died there in 1968. The house at 23 King Street is privately owned, but can be viewed from the street. Near it is the King Street United Church of Christ. Rose became active in the community life of this church; her memorial service was held there after her death.

LIBRARIES

Detroit Public Library (www.detroitpubliclibrary.org) was the first library in the world to name a branch for Laura Ingalls

Rose's town house in San Francisco

Wilder. Laura did not attend the 1949 dedication ceremonies, but she donated several important Little House memorabilia, including penciled manuscripts for *The Long Winter* and *These Happy Golden Years*, her schoolbooks, and original Sewell-Boyle illustrations from early editions of the Little House books. The Wilder Collection is permanently housed in the Detroit Public Library (5201 Woodward Ave., Detroit, MI 48202; tel. 313-833-1000). Open Tues.–Sun., 1 to 5. The **Wilder Branch** itself moved into new quarters in time to celebrate Laura's birthday centennial in 1967, and is now located at 7140 E. Seven Mile Road, Detroit, MI 48234. No exhibits or memorabilia are kept there, but metal artwork in the courtyard depicts artist Narendra Patel's interpretation of *Little House in the Big Woods.*

Pomona Public Library (P.O. Box 2271, 625 S. Garey Ave., Pomona, CA 91769; tel. 906-620-2043) dedicated a Laura Ingalls Wilder Room in 1950. Open Mon.–Thurs., 9 to 8, and Fri. and Sat., 12 to 5. The library has a permanent exhibit space displaying various Little House memorabilia, including the original manuscript of *Little Town on the Prairie*, presented by Laura. An annual Little House celebration at the library is the **Gingerbread Sociable**, held on the first Saturday in February, in honor of Laura's birthday. Laura was born on February 7.

Iowa Braille and Sight Saving School, located in Vinton, Iowa, was called the "Iowa College for the Blind" in the Little House books. Mary Ingalls enrolled there in 1881 and graduated in 1889. The historic old Main Building, which now is the center of the campus, was the structure Mary knew when she was a student there. The school maintains no special exhibits on Mary Ingalls.

INDEX

Page numbers in *italics* indicate illustrations.